Comedic Canvas Painting

Comedic Canvas Painting

Smiles with Stories

Olivia K

UNIEK ENTERPRISES

CONTENTS

Table of Content

Chapter 1

The Art of Humor

The craft of humor, an enrapturing and multi-layered feature of human articulation, rises above simple giggling, venturing into the profundities of our shared perspective to enlighten the human experience. From the earliest types of comedic articulation to contemporary indications, humor has filled in as a mirror reflecting society, a demulcent for the spirit, and an impetus for association. This investigation of the specialty of humor attempts to unwind its intricacies, following its verifiable roots, looking at its different structures, and diving into its significant effect on people and social orders.

Verifiable Underlying foundations of Humor:

The foundations of humor can be followed to the beginning of human correspondence, where giggling arose as a crude type of social holding. As people group shaped, humor developed into an instrument for common perspective, making a feeling of solidarity through shared entertainment. Old societies, like those of Greece and Rome, perceived the remedial worth of humor and consolidated comedic components into dramatic exhibitions, molding the establishment for the craft of humor as a social and social power.

From the beginning of time, humor has frequently tracked down a home in parody, a type of articulation that utilizes mind and incongruity to study cultural standards and human weaknesses. The plays of Aristophanes in old Greece and the sarcastic works of Juvenal in old Rome represent how humor has been used as a weapon of social critique, uncovering the idiocies and treacheries of their particular social orders. The Medieval times saw the rise of court jokesters, who utilized humor to explore the intricacies of regal courts, frequently filling in as truth-tellers shrouded jokingly.

The Renaissance time frame saw a recovery of interest in traditional writing and reasoning, prompting the joining of humor into different imaginative structures. William Shakespeare, an illuminator of the Renaissance, excelled at mixing misfortune and satire in his plays, exhibiting the duality of the human experience. Shakespeare's clever pleasantry, significant characters, and comedic components added to the persevering through allure of humor in writing and theater.

Different Types of Humor:

The craft of humor traverses a tremendous range, enveloping a bunch of structures and styles that take care of different preferences and sensibilities. From droll and joke to parody and incorrigible humor, every sign of humor carries its own remarkable flavor to the material of human articulation.

Droll and Actual Satire: At its generally essential level, humor frequently includes the component of shock, and actual parody, typified by droll, depends on overstated activities, flummoxes, and visual gags to inspire chuckling. This type of humor, pervasive in vaudeville, quiet movies, and exemplary sitcoms, addresses our natural appreciation for the ludicrous and the unforeseen.

Parody and Social Editorial: Humor turns into a powerful device for social study as parody. Ironical parody, set apart by smart pleasantry and incongruity, uncovered the inadequacies of people, establishments, and cultural standards. Parody welcomes us to giggle at the imprudences of humankind while empowering basic reflection on the condition of the world.

Mind and Wit: Verbal smoothness and cunning wit have for quite some time been praised in the realm of humor. Jokes, risqué statements, and etymological trapeze artistry stimulate the acumen, welcoming crowds to delight in the smart control of language. Crafted by Oscar Wilde and Stamp Twain embody the specialty of mind, where humor is unpredictably woven into the texture of articulate writing.

Incorrigible Humor: A more nuanced and dubious feature of humor arises as potentially offensive humor, which faces untouchable subjects and pushes the limits of cultural standards. Frequently portrayed by its disrespectfulness and readiness to investigate the ghastly, incorrigible humor welcomes crowds to find giggling notwithstanding life's gravest real factors, testing our discernments and safe places.

Absurdism and Oddity: The twentieth century saw the ascent of comedic structures that embraced the ludicrous and the dreamlike. Absurdist plays, similar to those of Samuel Beckett, defy the existential silliness of human life with humor. Surrealist humor, as exemplified by crafted by Salvador Dalí, investigates the peculiar and fantastical, testing the requirements of the real world.

Improvisational Satire: The immediacy of improvisational parody, frequently seen in improvisational theater and comedic ad lib shows, depends on speedy reasoning, joint effort, and crowd commitment. Comedy grandstands the craft of reasoning on one's feet, making giggling through unscripted and capricious minutes.

Humor as a Social Mirror:

The specialty of humor is a social mirror that mirrors the qualities, standards, and mannerisms of social orders since the beginning of time. Comedic articulations are well established in social settings, filling in as an impression of cultural mentalities, difficulties, and changes.

Humor turns into a powerful vehicle for testing cultural standards and cultivating social change. Since the beginning of time, joke artists, comedians, and comedians have employed their specialty to resolve issues of shamefulness, disparity, and political defilement. In the domain of stand-up parody, figures like Richard Pryor, George Carlin, and Joan Streams have involved humor for the purpose of social scrutinize, provoking crowds to reevaluate their points of view on disagreeable issues.

Besides, social and semantic subtleties shape the comedic scene. What might be diverting in one culture may be lost in interpretation in another. Culturally diverse trades of humor uncover the complexities of human correspondence, accentuating the significance of setting and shared encounters in comedic appreciation.

In contemporary society, computerized stages have democratized the creation and scattering of humor. Images, viral recordings, and virtual entertainment posts act as contemporary materials for comedic articulation, offering a worldwide stage for comedians to draw in with different crowds. Web humor mirrors the quickly developing nature of social references and cultural patterns, making a dynamic and steadily evolving scene.

The Recuperating Force of Chuckling:

Past its job as diversion and social editorial, the craft of humor has a significant remedial quality. Giggling, frequently alluded to as "the best medication," has obvious physical and mental advantages. The demonstration of giggling triggers the arrival of endorphins, the body's regular happy go lucky synthetic compounds, adding to a feeling of prosperity and briefly reducing torment.

In the domain of brain research, humor treatment tackles the recuperating force of giggling to advance psychological wellness and profound prosperity. Specialists use humor as a remedial device, perceiving its capacity to mitigate pressure, diminish tension, and cultivate an inspirational perspective. Giggling yoga, a training that consolidates deliberate chuckling practices with yogic standards, epitomizes the purposeful utilization of humor as an all encompassing way to deal with wellbeing and health.

The Development of Parody in Mainstream society:

Satire's advancement in mainstream society mirrors the moving elements of cultural standards and the changing scene of amusement. From the vaudeville phases of the mid twentieth hundred years to the sitcoms of the TV time and the ascent of advanced content, comedic articulations have adjusted to new mediums and crowd assumptions.

TV, specifically, plays had a vital impact in molding comedic sensibilities. Exemplary sitcoms like "I Love Lucy" and "Seinfeld" made ready for creative ways to deal with humor, while contemporary series like "The Workplace" and "Fleabag" challenge conventional comedic designs, embracing a more nuanced and complex narrating approach.

The stand-up parody scene has likewise gone through a renaissance, with entertainers investigating a great many individual and social points. The variety of voices and points of view in stand-up parody mirrors an expanded consciousness of the significance of portrayal and inclusivity in humor.

Computerized stages have democratized comedic creation, permitting entertainers to contact worldwide crowds with remarkable speed. Online substance makers, from jokesters to artists, have tracked down new roads for displaying their comedic abilities, with stages like YouTube and TikTok filling in as virtual stages for the up and coming age of comedians.

1.1 Exploring Different Forms of Comedy

Investigating the different types of satire uncovers a rich embroidery of comedic articulations that have developed over hundreds of years, adjusting to social movements, creative developments, and changing crowd sensibilities.

From the old venues of Greece to the computerized foundation of the 21st 100 years, parody has appeared in different types and styles, each offering a one of a kind point of view on the human experience. This investigation digs into various types of satire, looking at their qualities, verifiable roots, and persevering through advance.

1. **Droll Parody:**

   One of the earliest and most actual types of parody is droll, portrayed by misrepresented, rowdy activities and visual gags. Beginning from the Italian Commedia dell'arte and promoted in early quiet movies, droll depends on actual humor, flummoxes, and comedic timing to create chuckling. The Three Saps, Charlie Chaplin, and Buster Keaton are notorious figures related with droll, utilizing droll's tumultuous energy to engage crowds and rise above language hindrances. This type of satire requests to our basic impulses, inspiring chuckling through the widespread language of rawness and shock.

2. **Ironical Satire:**

   Ironical satire fills in as a sharp and frequently gnawing editorial on cultural standards, legislative issues, and human way of behaving. Tracing all the way back to old Greece with Aristophanes' ironical plays, this type of parody utilizes mind, incongruity, and misrepresentation to uncover the defects and idiocies of people and establishments. Quick's "Gulliver's Movements" and Voltaire's "Candide" epitomize scholarly parody, while present day humorists like Jon Stewart and John Oliver use TV as a stage to evaluate contemporary issues. Ironical parody shakes things up, provoking reflection and igniting discussions about cultural weaknesses.

3. **Mind and Wit:**

   Mind and wit structure the foundation of a more cerebral and etymological style of satire. Spearheaded by scholars like Oscar Wilde and Imprint Twain, this type of satire depends on smart wit, jokes, and phonetic trapeze artistry to entertain crowds. The humor frequently lies in the risqué statements, conundrums, and phonetic subtleties, welcoming the crowd to delight in the smart control of language. This type of satire is a demonstration of the creativity of language, where mind turns into a vehicle for both humor and scholarly commitment.

4. **Stand-Up Satire:**

Stand-up satire has arisen as an unmistakable and compelling type of comedic articulation, where jokesters act before a live crowd, frequently conveying a speech loaded up with observational humor, individual tales, and social editorial. The stand-up satire custom has establishes in vaudeville and has developed through illuminating presences like Richard Pryor, George Carlin, and Joan Streams. Today, different voices in stand-up, like Hannah Gadsby and Ali Wong, challenge shows and investigate many subjects, from individual encounters to social issues. Stand-up parody offers a personal and direct association between the joke artist and the crowd, depending on the appeal, timing, and narrating ability of the entertainer.

5. **Dim Parody:**

Dim parody explores the shocking, the untouchable, and the awkward with humor. It is portrayed by its readiness to investigate bleak or no subjects, finding giggling in circumstances that may be thought of as terrible. Essayists like Joseph Heller with "Impasse" and movies like "Dr. Strangelove" embody the mixing of incorrigible humor with serious topics. Comics like Louis C.K. what's more, Sarah Silverman have pushed the limits of worthiness, involving dull parody for of going up against awkward insights and testing cultural standards. Dull satire is a trying investigation of the scarce difference among misfortune and humor, compelling crowds to stand up to awkward insights through chuckling.

6. **Strange and Absurdist Satire:**

Strange and absurdist satire take a takeoff from the real world, embracing the odd, the silly, and the fantastical. Arising in the twentieth hundred years with developments like Dadaism and Oddity, specialists like Salvador Dalí and writers like Samuel Beckett used idiocy to mirror the bedlam and vulnerability of the advanced world. Comedic films as python Monty's "The

Sacred goal" and Programs like "Twin Pinnacles" have embraced the ludicrous, testing story shows and drawing in crowds in strange, fanciful scenes. Dreamlike satire welcomes watchers to address reality, revel in the strange, and track down humor in the unforeseen.

7. **Improvisational Satire:**

Improvisational satire, or comedy, is a type of unscripted execution where humorists cause situations and discourse precipitously. Established in performance center games and activities, comedy depends on speedy reasoning, coordinated effort, and crowd ideas to create humor. Shows like "Whose Line Is It In any case?" grandstand the comedic ability of improvisational entertainers, who explore capricious situations with mind and imagination. The intrinsic eccentricism of comedy makes a one of a kind and intelligent comedic experience, as entertainers and crowd the same find the humor continuously.

8. **Satire in Film and TV:**

The appearance of film and TV has given a visual stage to comedic articulation, permitting movie producers and showrunners to explore different avenues regarding different comedic structures. From exemplary quiet movies as chaplin Charlie's "City Lights" to the complex humor of TV series like "The Simpsons" and "Check Your Energy," visual media has turned into a jungle gym for comedic development. The mixing of visual gags, clever discourse, and story humor has made getting through comedic works of art that engage crowds across ages.

9. **Advanced Parody:**

The computerized age has introduced new roads for comedic articulation, with online stages filling in as a virtual stage for a different cluster of comics, content makers, and comedians. Images, viral recordings, and virtual entertainment posts have become present day vehicles for spreading humor internationally, with web culture molding the comedic scene.

Online joke artists, like those on YouTube and TikTok, have tracked down imaginative ways of drawing in with crowds, try different things with comedic organizes, and investigate specialty humor that resounds with explicit web-based networks. The computerized domain has democratized comedic creation, offering a unique space for arising gifts to exhibit their humor and interface with a worldwide crowd.

1. **Stand-up Comedy**

   Stand-up satire, a cozy and direct type of comedic articulation, has arisen as a conspicuous and compelling medium, dazzling crowds with its mix of observational humor, individual stories, and social editorial. Established in vaudeville and sharpened through the ages by comedic illuminating presences, stand-up satire has developed into a dynamic and various fine art that rises above social limits and talks straightforwardly to the human experience.

   At its center, stand-up satire is an independent presentation where a comic stands before a live crowd, outfitted exclusively with a mouthpiece and their mind, conveying a talk expected to incite giggling. This unadorned arrangement puts the joke artist in direct correspondence with the crowd, making a prompt and instinctive association that recognizes stand-up from other comedic structures.

   The starting points of stand-up parody can be followed back to vaudeville, where entertainers would convey comedic talks as a feature of a theatrical presentation. Nonetheless, it was during the twentieth century that stand-up parody arose as a particular work of art, with entertainers like Lenny Bruce and Mort Sahl spearheading a more conversational and socially cognizant style. Bruce, specifically, pushed the limits of satisfactory talk, utilizing stand-up as a stage for provocative social critique and parody.

As stand-up satire kept on developing, the 1970s and 1980s saw the ascent of comedic legends who became inseparable from the work of art. Richard Pryor's crude and confession booth narrating, George Carlin's sharp friendly evaluates, and Joan Streams' exploring mind helped shape the scene of stand-up satire. These trailblazers prepared for people in the future as well as exhibited the force of stand-up for of going up against cultural standards and thinking about the human condition.

One of the characterizing highlights of stand-up satire is its capacity to distil the commonplace and the ridiculous parts of daily existence into appealing and entertaining stories. Humorists frequently draw motivation from their own encounters, offering an individual focal point through which the crowd can see the world. Whether investigating relational intricacies, connections, or the peculiarities of present day living, stand-up satire changes the normal into the exceptional through the speculative chemistry of chuckling.

Observational humor, a sign of stand-up, includes distinctly noticing the world and introducing it through a comedic focal point. Jerry Seinfeld, known for his observational ability, makes humor from the small details of day to day existence, transforming the apparently insignificant into wellsprings of chuckling. From the characteristics of social decorum to the idiocies of innovation, observational jokesters find humor in the common encounters that associate all of us.

The conveyance style of professional comics is basically as significant as the actual substance. The specialty of timing, pacing, and the utilization of stops are fundamental parts that add to the viability of a stand-up everyday practice. A very much coordinated zinger or an impeccably executed delay can uplift the effect of a joke, making a cadence that keeps the crowd locked in. The genuineness of the jokester, their signals, and looks likewise assume a part in conveying humor and upgrading the general presentation.

Stand-up satire is a dynamic and versatile fine art, permitting entertainers to investigate a large number of points, from the cheerful to the significant. While certain comics succeed at creating jokes that incite chortles, others use humor as a vehicle for social critique, handling issues like legislative issues, race, and orientation. The capacity of stand-up satire to explore the range of human experience gives it a novel flexibility that resounds with different crowds.

The democratization of stand-up parody has been worked with by satire clubs, open mic evenings, and the multiplication of online stages. Satire clubs act as hatcheries for arising ability, giving a space to jokesters to sharpen their specialty, test material, and interface with crowds in a close setting. Open mic evenings offer hopeful joke artists the chance to step onto the stage, share their viewpoint, and refine their comedic voice.

Lately, online stages have changed the scene of stand-up parody, empowering joke artists to contact worldwide crowds without the limitations of customary guardians. Stages like Netflix, YouTube, and web-based entertainment have become platforms for jokesters to grandstand their specials, cuts, and comedic personas. The openness of computerized stages has democratized comedic perceivability, permitting comics from different foundations and locales to track down crowds on a worldwide scale.

The variety of voices in stand-up parody has extended fundamentally, testing customary standards and widening the scope of viewpoints addressed in front of an audience. Comics from minimized networks, including ladies, ethnic minorities, and LGBTQ+ people, are utilizing stand-up as a stage to share their one of a kind encounters and challenge generalizations. This enhancement of voices improves the comedic scene as well as adds to a more comprehensive and delegate type of diversion.

Be that as it may, the advancement of stand-up parody has not been without its difficulties. The limits of OK humor are constantly tried, and comics frequently wind up exploring the fragile harmony between stretching the limits and staying away from offense.

Discussions encompassing the fittingness of specific jokes, especially those connected with touchy subjects, highlight the continuous discussion about the obligation and effect of parody in contemporary society.

The effect of stand-up satire stretches out past the stage and screen; it impacts cultural talk, challenges standards, and gives a soothing delivery to crowds. Through humor, jokesters offer a focal point through which to view and scrutinize the world, frequently provoking basic reflection on friendly issues. Professional comics become social pundits, deciphering the general outlook and giving crowds a common space for chuckling and consideration.

2. Satire

Parody, a type of humor that utilizes incongruity, mind, and embellishment to reprimand and taunt cultural indecencies, has for quite some time been an intense instrument for social editorial. Established in old practices, parody has persevered through the ages as a vehicle for dispute, evaluate, and reflection. This investigation of parody digs into its verifiable roots, qualities, and its getting through job as a mirror mirroring the imprudences and idiocies of society.

Verifiable Roots:

The foundations of parody can be followed back to old Greece, where Aristophanes, a comic dramatist, utilized parody in his plays to parody political figures, savvy people, and cultural standards. Nonetheless, it was during the Roman period that parody really prospered, outstandingly with crafted by Horace and Juvenal. Juvenalian parody, named after the Roman writer Juvenal, is described by its cruel and severe evaluate of cultural defilement, making it an intense type of parody that holds a mirror to the haziest parts of humankind.

In the Medieval times, mocking components tracked down articulation in progress of Geoffrey Chaucer, especially in "The Canterbury Stories," where he evaluated the bad faith and moral shortfalls of different social classes. The Renaissance saw the recovery of traditional writing, and ironical works as swift Jonathan's "A Humble Proposition" utilized incongruity and misrepresentation to condemn English strategies and the treatment of the Irish.

Qualities of Parody:

At its center, parody is described by its utilization of humor, incongruity, misrepresentation, and scorn to reprimand and deride people, establishments, or cultural shows. Parody frequently utilizes mind and sharp pleasantry, involving humor as a rebellious device to uncover lip service, defilement, and cultural weaknesses.

Two essential types of parody have arisen over the long run: Horatian and Juvenalian. Horatian parody, named after the Roman artist Horace, is more delicate and happy. It intends to entertain and address with a grin instead of a frown, frequently taking on a perky tone to energize reflection as opposed to cruel analysis. Then again, Juvenalian parody is gnawing, basic, and frequently more forceful, trying to uncover and censure cultural wrongs with an immediate and harsh methodology.

Parody can appear in different mediums, including writing, theater, visual expressions, and all the more as of late, in TV and online substance. Humorous writing frequently appears as books, articles, or sonnets, with writers utilizing fictitious settings or characters to evaluate genuine issues. Mocking plays, similar to Molière's "Fraud," utilize dramatic components to feature cultural idiocies and cause to notice human indiscretion.

Visual parody, particularly predominant in political kid's shows and exaggerations, utilizes pictures to convey studies with a punch. Ironical kid's shows frequently utilize misrepresented highlights to deride people of note, legislators, or cultural patterns, giving an outwardly significant type of discourse.

Political Parody:

One of the most pervasive and getting through types of parody is political parody. In the midst of political strife or social commotion, humorists have used their pens to parody legislators, legislatures, and power structures. Jonathan Quick's "Gulliver's Movements," for instance, utilizes a fantastical story to ridicule political debasement, human instinct, and cultural orders.

In the domain of political kid's shows, craftsmen like Honore Daumier and George Cruikshank involved their outlines to condemn the political foundation in the nineteenth hundred years. In later times, political parody has found a home in TV programs like "Saturday Night Live," "The Day to day Show," and "Last Week This evening," where comics use parody to take apart recent developments, strategies, and political figures.

Ironical parody on TV gives diversion as well as fills in as a critical wellspring of data for watchers. Entertainers like John Oliver and Jon Stewart use parody to break down complex issues, introducing them in an edible and comical configuration that energizes decisive reasoning and urban commitment.

Social Parody:

Past governmental issues, parody is a flexible device for investigating different parts of society, including normal practices, social practices, and human way of behaving. Oscar Wilde's "The Significance of Being Sincere" mocks Victorian social mores and the quest for marriage. In current writing, Kurt Vonnegut's "Feline's Support" utilizes silliness and parody to look at the risks of uncontrolled logical advancement and atomic multiplication.

Social parody frequently plans to uncover the idiocies and logical inconsistencies intrinsic in cultural designs. It challenges standards, questions customs, and prompts crowds to reexamine their suspicions about their general surroundings. Through humor, social parody offers a focal point through which to see cultural inadequacies, encouraging a feeling of reflection and, on occasion, uneasiness.

Parody in the Computerized Age:

The computerized age has led to another period of parody, with online stages giving a democratized space to humorists and jokesters to contact worldwide crowds. Ironical sites, sarcastic news shows, and virtual entertainment accounts use humor to remark on recent developments, mainstream society, and cultural patterns.

Online stages have permitted humorists to contact assorted crowds and deal elective points of view on news and issues. The ascent of humorous media sources, for example, "The Onion" and "The Day to day Squash," obscures the lines among fiction and reality, provoking perusers to observe between certified news and sarcastic editorial.

Web-based entertainment stages, especially Twitter, have become amazing assets for humorists to disperse their studies rapidly and generally. Images, a type of sarcastic visual correspondence, consolidate complex thoughts into shareable and hilarious pictures, making them a successful method for scattering mocking discourse.

Nonetheless, the computerized age additionally presents difficulties for parody. The speed of data scattering can prompt errors, and humorous substance can be taken inappropriately, prompting potentially negative results. Also, the closed quarters nature of web-based entertainment can bring about parody being consumed basically by similar crowds, restricting testing assorted perspectives potential.

Difficulties and Discussions:

Parody, by its inclination, is provocative, and its ability to challenge authority and cultural standards frequently prompts contention. Comedians walk a barely recognizable difference between giving gnawing social critique and possibly culpable or distancing their crowd. The emotional idea of humor makes it trying to foresee how various people or gatherings will see parody.

Lately, conversations about social awareness, allotment, and the potential damage brought about by specific types of parody have come to the very front. Parody that sustains hurtful generalizations, derides minimized gatherings, or builds up existing power irregular characteristics brings up moral issues about the obligation of comedians and the likely effect of their work on society.

Regardless of these difficulties, parody stays a fundamental and effective type of articulation that supports decisive reasoning, challenges authority, and gives a soothing delivery to people exploring the intricacies of the cutting edge world.

3. Slapstick

Droll, an immortal and boisterous type of parody, has been a staple in diversion for quite a long time, spellbinding crowds with its rawness, distortion, and ageless allure. Established in dramatic practices and advancing through vaudeville, quiet movies, and then some, droll parody rises above language obstructions, depending on the general language of actual humor to incite chuckling. This investigation of droll digs into its authentic roots, qualities, and persevering through notoriety.

Authentic Roots:

The starting points of droll can be followed back to antiquated dramatic customs, where actual parody and overstated signals were indispensable pieces of exhibitions. Notwithstanding, the expression "droll" itself finds its foundations in the Commedia dell'arte, an Italian type of improvisational theater that thrived in the sixteenth to eighteenth hundreds of years. Commedia dell'arte included stock characters, and the "droll" was a prop — an oar with two pieces that rushed out with an uproarious sound, adding accentuation to actual activities.

The change from Commedia dell'arte to droll as far as we might be concerned today happened in the domain of vaudeville in the late nineteenth and mid twentieth hundreds of years. Vaudeville entertainers, trying to engage different crowds, integrated droll components into their demonstrations, frequently highlighting overstated actual activities, flummoxes, and visual gags to inspire chuckling. Quiet film stars like Charlie Chaplin, Buster Keaton, and Harold Lloyd further promoted droll, bringing its extraordinary kind of actual parody to a worldwide crowd.

Qualities of Droll:

Droll satire is portrayed by its dependence on actual humor, overstated activities, and silly circumstances. It frequently includes components, for example, flummoxes, pie tossing, droll viciousness, and visual gags that play on the startling and the crazy. The humor in droll emerges from the mishap or awkwardness of characters, transforming common circumstances into wellsprings of giggling.

A critical component of droll is its effortlessness and openness. The genuineness of the parody permits it to rise above language boundaries, making it all around engaging. Whether in the excited speed of a quiet film or the very much arranged schedules of a live exhibition, droll catches the embodiment of humor through activity and response.

Droll frequently depends on the utilization of stock characters, each with unmistakable qualities that add to the comedic dynamic. The blundering fool, the straight man, and the devilish comedian are models that track down their direction into droll situations, each adding to the mayhem and giggling in their own particular manner.

Quiet Film Time:

The quiet film time, frequently viewed as the brilliant period of droll, saw the ascent of notable jokesters who became inseparable from the class. Charlie Chaplin, with his notable Drifter character, utilized actual parody to feature the battles of the everyday person in a quickly impacting world. Buster Keaton, known for his stone-colored articulation and noteworthy trick work, made visual gags that stay celebrated for their advancement and humor.

Harold Lloyd, another quiet film star, mixed droll with sharp narrating, making many-sided comedic accounts. His clock-hanging scene in "Wellbeing Last!" is an exemplary illustration of how droll can make strain through actual danger while creating giggling from the crowd.

The visual idea of quiet movies permitted droll jokesters to grandstand their actual ability without the requirement for exchange. Expressive looks, overstated motions, and beautifully coordinated activities turned into the language of droll, enthralling crowds and laying out its persevering through prevalence.

Vaudeville and Live Execution:

In the vaudeville time, live exhibitions carried droll to the stage, highlighting comedic pairs, jokesters, and actual comics who connected straightforwardly with the crowd. The Three Chumps, a vaudeville-enlivened satire group, acquired notoriety for their droll tricks, integrating eye-jabs, face slaps, and comedic viciousness into their schedules.

Vaudeville entertainers adjusted to various crowd inclinations, joining droll with music, dance, and assortment acts. The instantaneousness of live execution permitted droll comics to communicate straightforwardly with their crowd, making an enthusiastic and drawing in experience that added to the class' getting through fame.

Present day Impact and Variations:

While droll's prime might be related with the mid twentieth 100 years, its impact perseveres in present day parody. The actual parody of entertainers like Jim Carrey and Rowan Atkinson (Mr. Bean) mirrors the persevering through allure of droll. Carrey's flexible looks and Atkinson's quiet and expressive humor give proper respect to the exemplary components of droll.

Vivified kid's shows, especially those delivered by studios like Warner Brothers. what's more, Hanna-Barbera, have embraced droll practices. The overstated activities of characters like Bugs Rabbit and Tom and Jerry draw motivation from the rawness and visual gags of exemplary droll.

The impact of droll stretches out to contemporary sitcoms and satire films. While exchange and clever talk assume a huge part, numerous comedies consolidate droll components to enhance the humor. From abnormal actual experiences to expand flummoxes, droll keeps on being a flexible and powerful comedic device in different types of diversion.

Reactions and Debates:

While droll is commended for its widespread allure and getting through giggling, it isn't without reactions. A few contend that the actual savagery and flummoxes frequently connected with droll can propagate destructive generalizations or standardize forceful way of behaving. The droll savagery coordinated at specific characters, especially in early kid's shows, possibly affects youthful crowds.

Also, pundits contend that droll can be standard, depending on monotonous gags and unsurprising situations. The straightforwardness that makes droll open can likewise be a limit, prompting allegations of triviality and absence of profundity in comedic narrating.

1.2 The Psychology of Laughter

The brain science of chuckling is an entrancing investigation into the complicated manners by which humor impacts the human psyche and conduct. Giggling, frequently viewed as the widespread language of bliss, fills in as a complicated social and mental peculiarity well established in human development, correspondence, and close to home prosperity.

Transformative Viewpoint:

From a transformative viewpoint, giggling is accepted to have begun as a social holding component among early people. Shared chuckling inside a gathering probably filled in as a sign of security and kinship, supporting social bonds and advancing collaboration. The capacity to find humor in specific circumstances might enjoy gave transformative benefits, encouraging gathering union and correspondence.

The developmental underlying foundations of chuckling are apparent in non-human primates, where perky ways of behaving and vocalizations similar to human giggling can be noticed. This common quality across species recommends that chuckling serves principal capabilities in friendly connections, originating before the improvement of language.

Social Holding and Correspondence:

In contemporary society, chuckling keeps on assuming a vital part in friendly holding and correspondence. Shared giggling upgrades relational associations, encouraging a feeling of solidarity and common comprehension. It goes about as a social grease, separating boundaries and laying out compatibility among people.

Besides, chuckling is exceptionally infectious, working as a type of nonverbal correspondence that rises above language obstructions. The sound of giggling triggers reflect neurons in the mind, prompting an unconstrained craving to participate in the chuckling, even without direct comprehension of the joke or circumstance. This infectious nature of giggling adds to the formation of shared encounters and a feeling of having a place inside gatherings.

Mental and Physiological Advantages:

Giggling isn't just a social device; it likewise offers a heap of mental and physiological advantages. According to a mental point of view, giggling is a strong pressure minimizer. The demonstration of snickering triggers the arrival of endorphins, the body's normal warm hearted synthetics, advancing a general feeling of prosperity and unwinding.

Moreover, giggling invigorates the creation of serotonin, a synapse related with state of mind guideline. The mental effect of giggling stretches out to its capacity to reduce uneasiness, raise state of mind, and briefly shift people's concentrate away from stressors. In helpful settings, giggling treatment has arisen as a comprehensive way to deal with working on psychological well-being, lessening pressure, and advancing profound versatility.

On a physiological level, chuckling prompts changes in the body that add to further developed wellbeing. It increments blood stream, upgrades cardiovascular capability, and further develops safe framework reactions. Ordinary chuckling has been related with lower levels of pressure chemicals, possibly decreasing the gamble of pressure related ailments. The coordination of chuckling into medical services rehearses highlights its true capacity as a corresponding instrument for advancing in general prosperity.

Mental Parts of Humor:

The mental parts of humor assume a vital part in the brain research of chuckling. Humor frequently includes confusion, shock, or the infringement of assumptions. The mind's capacity to perceive and value these components adds to the experience of tracking down something interesting. The confusion hypothesis of humor places that giggling emerges when there is an unexpected change in understanding or assumption, making a mental disharmony that is settled through chuckling.

Besides, humor frequently includes a pun, risqué statements, or smart etymological developments. This phonetic part of humor connects with mental cycles connected with language understanding and translation. The cerebrum's capacity to process and value phonetic subtleties adds to the mental delight got from jokes and comedic articulations.

The improvement of a comical inclination is a perplexing interaction of mental, social, and social elements. It develops throughout the span of a singular's life, formed by encounters, social impacts, and social associations.

While certain parts of humor are general, others are socially unambiguous, mirroring the variety in the ways various social orders express and appreciate comedic components.

Humor as Strategy for dealing with stress:

Giggling likewise fills in as a survival technique, permitting people to explore and adapt to life's difficulties. Humor, especially despite misfortune, can give a mental cradle, empowering people to reexamine circumstances, track down significance in challenges, and keep a feeling of versatility. This versatile capability of humor is apparent in different helpful methodologies, including humor treatment and chuckling yoga, which saddle the positive mental and physiological impacts of giggling for restorative purposes.

The mental rebuilding worked with by humor can impact a singular's point of view on stressors, cultivating a more hopeful standpoint. This mental reappraisal is connected to expanded mental adaptability, empowering people to move toward hardships with more noteworthy versatility and close to home guideline.

Individual Contrasts in Humor:

Notwithstanding the widespread idea of giggling, there are critical individual contrasts in the discernment and enthusiasm for humor. Factors like character, social foundation, and educational encounters add to the variety in comedic inclinations. The idea of a "comical inclination" envelops a singular's capacity to perceive, appreciate, and make humor.

Character qualities, for example, receptiveness to encounter and a proclivity for oddity, impact a singular's openness to various types of humor. Social foundation assumes a critical part, forming the kinds of humor that are viewed as satisfactory or no inside a given society. Educational encounters, including openness to different types of media, social associations, and individual difficulties, add to the advancement of a singular's novel awareness of what's actually funny.

1. **Why We Laugh**

    The peculiarity of chuckling, profoundly imbued in the human experience, fills in as a captivating investigation of our brain science, social elements, and developmental history. Understanding the reason why we giggle requires digging into the intricate interchange of physiological, mental, and social factors that add to this general articulation of euphoria and entertainment.

    Transformative Roots:

    Chuckling's transformative starting points can be followed back to our precursors as a social holding system. Early people, living in affectionate gatherings, possible involved giggling as a nonverbal sign of wellbeing, shared insight, and kinship.

With regards to advancement, chuckling may have worked with social union, reinforcing relational associations and cultivating collaboration inside gatherings.

The transformative foundations of giggling are apparent in different primates, where energy, vocalizations looking like chuckling, and shared articulations of satisfaction are noticed. This coherence across species highlights the key job of chuckling in friendly holding and correspondence, originating before the advancement of mind boggling language.

Physiological Premise:

Giggling isn't just a mental reaction; it significantly affects the body's physiology. At the point when we giggle, our mind discharges endorphins, the body's regular happy go lucky synthetic compounds, initiating a feeling of delight and bliss. This physiological reaction adds to the general feeling of prosperity related with chuckling.

Besides, chuckling has been connected to the initiation of the ventromedial prefrontal cortex, a cerebrum district related with remuneration handling. The cerebrum's prize framework builds up ways of behaving that add to endurance and social union, giving a neurobiological premise to the developmentally versatile nature of chuckling.

The demonstration of giggling likewise invigorates the arrival of dopamine, a synapse related with joy and support. This neurochemical overflow adds to the uplifting feedback of giggling, making a cycle that energizes social holding and the redundancy of chuckling initiating ways of behaving.

Mental Perspectives:

The mental parts of why we chuckle are complex, including processes connected with humor, shock, and social comprehension. Humor frequently emerges from disjointedness — circumstances where there is an unexpected change in understanding or assumption. The mind's capacity to perceive and value disjointed qualities adds to the mental delight got from jokes and comedic articulations.

Moreover, humor frequently includes shock, where the zinger or comedic component strays from assumptions. The component of shock draws in mental cycles related with expectation and example acknowledgment. The cerebrum's capacity to expect and afterward be shocked by a comedic curve adds a layer of mental intricacy to the experience of giggling.

Social comprehension assumes an essential part in why we snicker, particularly in friendly settings. Giggling fills in as a type of nonverbal correspondence, conveying a scope of social signs, including liveliness, acknowledgment, and mutual perspective. The capacity to perceive and answer these expressive gestures is profoundly implanted in human brain research and adds to the supporting idea of shared chuckling.

Social Capability:

At its center, chuckling is a significantly friendly way of behaving. Whether partook in a gathering or set off by friendly communications, chuckling supports social securities and works with positive associations among people. In group environments, chuckling goes about as a widespread language, rising above social and semantic contrasts.

Giggling is infectious, a peculiarity made sense of by reflect neurons in the cerebrum. The sound of chuckling triggers an unconstrained craving to participate, even without a trace of grasping the reason for the giggling. This infectious nature of chuckling fortifies social bonds, making a common encounter that adds to bunch union and a feeling of having a place.

Besides, chuckling fills in as a social grease, facilitating strain, separating social boundaries, and encouraging a positive air. In both easygoing collaborations and more conventional settings, the presence of chuckling frequently demonstrates a loose and harmonious social climate.

Survival strategy:

Giggling likewise works as a survival strategy, assisting people with exploring the difficulties and stresses of life. Humor, especially despite difficulty, permits people to reexamine circumstances, track down importance in hardships, and keep a feeling of flexibility. This versatile capability of giggling is clear in restorative methodologies like humor treatment and chuckling yoga, where deliberate chuckling is utilized to advance close to home prosperity.

The mental rebuilding worked with by humor can impact a singular's viewpoint on stressors, cultivating a more hopeful standpoint. This mental reappraisal is connected to expanded mental adaptability, empowering people to move toward hardships with more noteworthy versatility and profound guideline.

Individual and Social Contrasts:

While chuckling is a widespread human encounter, individual and social contrasts add to the variety in comedic inclinations and articulations of humor. Factors like character, social foundation, and educational encounters shape a singular's novel funny bone. Character qualities, for example, receptiveness to encounter and a proclivity for oddity, impact a singular's openness to various types of humor. Social foundation assumes a critical part, forming the sorts of humor that are viewed as satisfactory or no inside a given society. Valuable encounters, including openness to different types of media, social connections, and individual difficulties, add to the advancement of a singular's exceptional awareness of what's actually funny.

2. **Benefits of Laughter**

The advantages of chuckling stretch out a long ways past the quick euphoria and entertainment it brings. A powerful group of examination has enlightened the significant positive effect that chuckling has on physical, mental, and social prosperity. From decreasing pressure to improving cardiovascular wellbeing, chuckling fills in as a strong remedial device with a heap of advantages.

Stress Decrease:

One of the most deeply grounded advantages of chuckling is its job in pressure decrease. Chuckling triggers the arrival of endorphins, the body's normal lighthearted synthetic compounds, prompting a feeling of elation and unwinding. The physiological changes that go with chuckling, for example, diminished cortisol levels (a pressure chemical), add to a general decrease in pressure and strain.

Besides, chuckling instigates a condition of profound actual unwinding, easing muscle pressure and advancing a feeling of quiet. In upsetting circumstances, consolidating humor and tracking down motivations to chuckle can go about as a survival strategy, offering an important profound delivery and relieving the negative impacts of ongoing pressure.

Cardiovascular Wellbeing:

The cardiovascular advantages of chuckling are significant, as it has been displayed to affect heart wellbeing decidedly. Giggling advances vasodilation, the enlarging of veins, prompting expanded blood stream. This, thus, upgrades cardiovascular capability, further developing dissemination and possibly diminishing the gamble of cardiovascular infections.

Studies have shown the way that chuckling can prompt transient decreases in circulatory strain, a critical calculate keeping up with heart wellbeing. The cardiovascular advantages of chuckling are especially significant in the present speedy and frequently upsetting ways of life, where preventive measures against heart-related issues are critical.

Safe Framework Upgrade:

Chuckling has been connected to upgrades in the resistant framework, reinforcing the body's capacity to shield against diseases and sicknesses. The arrival of neuropeptides, little proteins that assist with managing safe reactions, is increased during giggling. Furthermore, chuckling expands the creation of safe cells and antibodies, adding to a more powerful and responsive resistant framework.

Research proposes that people who participate in exercises that prompt giggling might encounter a lift in resistant capability, making them less defenseless to normal diseases. This insusceptible upgrading impact highlights the all encompassing advantages of chuckling, lining up with the aphorism that "laughter is a pain killer with no side effects."

Torment The executives:

The restorative impacts of giggling reach out to torment the board, offering a characteristic and charming method for mitigating uneasiness. Chuckling triggers the arrival of endorphins, which add to temperament rise as well as go about as the body's normal pain relievers. People encountering torment or uneasiness frequently find help through chuckling, which can occupy from vibes of agony and advance a more certain mentality.

Giggling's aggravation easing properties have been seen in different clinical settings, with chuckling treatment earning respect as a corresponding methodology in torment the board procedures. Whether coordinated into medical care rehearses or embraced as an individual survival technique's, giggling skill to moderate the view of torment features its diverse remedial potential.

Mind-set Improvement and Emotional wellness:

Chuckling is a strong state of mind enhancer, equipped for cheer everyone up and encouraging a positive mental state. The arrival of endorphins and the decrease in pressure chemicals add to a superior state of mind and a feeling of prosperity. Chuckling likewise invigorates the development of serotonin, a synapse related with mind-set guideline and sensations of bliss.

In the domain of emotional wellness, giggling has been perceived as an important device in battling nervousness and wretchedness. The demonstration of snickering can hinder pessimistic idea designs, offering a transitory relief from close to home pain. Giggling treatment, an arising approach in emotional wellness treatment, use the positive mental and physiological impacts of chuckling to ease side effects of mind-set problems.

Social Association and Holding:

Giggling is a general language that rises above social and phonetic hindrances, encouraging social association and holding. Shared chuckling fortifies relational connections, making a feeling of solidarity and shared encounters. In group environments, giggling goes about as a strong social oil, separating boundaries, and advancing a positive and genial air.

The infectious idea of giggling, driven by reflect neurons in the cerebrum, supports overall vibes and upgrades social attachment. The capacity to partake in giggling develops a feeling of having a place and builds up the social texture inside families, networks, and bigger cultural settings.

Mental Advantages:

Chuckling connects with mental cycles, offering mental excitement and mental advantages. Humor frequently includes disjointedness, shock, and pleasantry, provoking the mind to perceive examples and make startling associations. The mental feeling given by humor adds to expanded imagination and mental adaptability.

Additionally, chuckling can work on mental capability by improving memory and consideration. Studies have shown that people who experience positive feelings, for example, those incited by chuckling, exhibit better mental execution. The mental advantages of chuckling feature its job in profound prosperity as well as in keeping up with and improving mental capacities over the long haul.

2

Chapter 2

Setting the Stage

Setting the stage is an essential part of any story, be it in writing, theater, film, or any type of narrating. The specialty of making a distinctive and vivid setting fills in as the establishment whereupon the whole story unfurls. Through cautious making of the climate, a creator or maker welcomes the crowd into a world rich with air, tone, and setting, laying out a background that upgrades the story and dazzles the creative mind.

Scholarly Setting:

In writing, the setting is something beyond an actual background; a fundamental component shapes the mind-set, impacts character conduct, and fills in as a representative space. Whether it's the ruined fields of Emily Brontë's "Wuthering Levels," the mysterious universe of J.K. Rowling's "Harry Potter" series, or the tragic regions of Suzanne Collins' "The Craving Games," the scholarly setting goes about as a person by its own doing, impacting the account and cooperating with the story's heroes.

The decision of setting is a conscious choice, mirroring the subjects and goals of the story. It gives the setting to the characters' encounters, forming their perspective and affecting their activities. A very much created scholarly setting transports perusers to various environments, permitting them to vicariously encounter the sights, sounds, and feelings that saturate the story.

Dramatic Setting:

In the domain of theater, the setting envelops actual components as well as the game plan of room, lighting, and sound. The stage fills in as a material where the story unfurls, and the set plan turns into a visual and tangible expansion of the story. Dramatic settings range from intricate, sensible portrayals to moderate, emblematic portrayals, each decided to supplement the subjects and tone of the play.

Theater blossoms with the quickness of the live exhibition, and the setting assumes a urgent part in submerging the crowd in the realm of the play. From the magnificence of Shakespearean stages to the personal moderation of contemporary creations, the setting establishes the vibe for the crowd's close to home commitment. It gives a visual and environmental setting that improves the effect of the story, making a common encounter between the entertainers and the crowd.

Film Setting:

In the domain of film, the setting takes on a visual aspect unmatched in its capacity to move watchers into substitute real factors. Movie producers use areas, set plan, cinematography, and enhanced visualizations to make vivid universes that upgrade the narrating experience. From the general scenes of sagas like "Lawrence of Arabia" to the claustrophobic spaceship insides of "Outsider," the film setting is a visual language that conveys tone, sort, and story purpose.

Film settings lay out the actual climate as well as add to the general stylish and environment of the story. The interaction of light and shadow, the selection of varieties, and the arrangement of each casing all add to the close to home reverberation of the story. The film setting is a dynamic and multi-layered component that shapes the crowd's discernment, directing their close to home reactions and improving the effect of the story.

Intuitive Setting:

In the domain of intuitive narrating, for example, computer games, the setting takes on an extra layer of importance. Players are not latent onlookers but rather dynamic members in the story, and the setting turns into a powerful space that answers player decisions and activities. Game engineers fastidiously plan conditions that work with investigation, disclosure, and commitment, permitting players to become submerged in the imaginary world.

Intuitive settings in computer games are in many cases sweeping and definite, empowering players to focus profoundly on investigating the subtleties of the climate. Whether it's the open-world scenes of games like "The Legend of Zelda: Breath of Nature" or the barometrical complexities of repulsiveness games like "Occupant Evil," the intuitive setting adds to the player's office and close to home interest in the account.

The Meaning of Setting:

Setting isn't only a scenery; it is a story gadget with significant ramifications for the story's subjects, character improvement, and in general effect. A very much created setting can inspire a particular state of mind, get close to home reactions, and convey topical propensities. Think about F. Scott Fitzgerald's "The Incomparable Gatsby," where the richness of the Thundering Twenties' setting fills in as a conspicuous difference to the ethical rot and disappointment at the core of the story.

Setting likewise assumes an essential part in laying out the social and verifiable setting of a story. It gives a focal point through which perusers or watchers can acquire bits of knowledge into the characters' lives and the cultural standards that shape their encounters. For instance, Isabel Allende's "The Place of the Spirits" utilizes the setting of Chile to wind around a story complicatedly laced with the country's political and social scene.

Besides, the setting goes about as an account anchor, establishing the story in a substantial reality. Whether it's the cutting edge oppressed world of George Orwell's "1984" or the capricious universe of Lewis Carroll's "Alice's Undertakings in Wonderland," the setting gives a structure that permits the crowd to suspend doubt and completely draw in with the story.

Difficulties and Contemplations:

Making a successful setting requires a cautious harmony among detail and vagueness. An excess of detail can overpower the crowd, smothering their creative mind and hindering their capacity to extend themselves into the story. Then again, too little detail can bring about a setting that needs profundity and neglects to drench the crowd completely.

Makers should likewise think about the social and verifiable setting of their setting, guaranteeing validness and keeping away from generalizations or deceptions. The setting ought to improve the story instead of act as a simple scenery, and its decisions ought to line up with the subjects and messages the maker means to pass on.

2.1 Creating Memorable Characters

Making important characters is a craftsmanship that goes past the simple demonstration of putting words on a page or carrying entertainers to a set. It includes a sensitive transaction of inventiveness, compassion, and a comprehension of the human condition. Whether in writing, film, theater, or any narrating medium, characters are the thumping heart of accounts, and their capacity to resound with crowds is fundamental. Making characters that wait in the personalities and hearts of perusers or watchers requires a smart and purposeful methodology.

Intricacy and Profundity:

Critical characters are many times set apart by their intricacy and profundity. They exist past basic prime examples or one-layered qualities, having an extravagance that reflects the complexities of genuine individuals. Think about the personality of Jay Gatsby in F. Scott Fitzgerald's "The Incomparable Gatsby." Gatsby isn't simply a rich man with a puzzling past; he is an image of the Pursuit of happiness, tormented by solitary love and a determined quest for a romanticized vision of progress.

Characters gain profundity through a blend of interior and outer struggles, defects, and temperances. An investigation of their past, inspirations, and wants permits crowds to interface with the characters on a more significant level. Imperfections, specifically, adapt characters, making them interesting and giving open doors to development and advancement all through the story.

Unmistakable Characters and Characteristics:

Noteworthy characters frequently have unmistakable characters and characteristics that put them aside. Whether it's Sherlock Holmes' sharp insightful capacities and unpredictable propensities or the quirks of Roald Dahl's Willy Wonka, these qualities become the person's mark, having an enduring impact on the crowd.

These idiosyncrasies can appear in different ways — unmistakable discourse designs, extraordinary actual attributes, or unpredictable ways of behaving. Consider the noteworthy person of Chief Jack Sparrow in Disney's "Privateers of the Caribbean" establishment. His slurred discourse, unusual peculiarities, and capricious activities make him particular as well as add to his appeal and charm.

Engaging Inspirations:

For characters to reverberate with crowds, their inspirations should be engaging in some way or another. Whether driven by adoration, desire, vengeance, or a mission for personality, the characters' objectives and wants ought to take advantage of widespread subjects and feelings. This appeal permits crowds to feel for the characters' excursions and put genuinely in their battles and wins.

The personality of Katniss Everdeen in Suzanne Collins' "The Craving Games" series represents this appeal. Katniss' essential inspiration is to safeguard her friends and family, a basic sense that resounds with perusers confronting their own difficulties and obligations. By establishing characters in engaging inspirations, makers fashion an association between the imaginary world and the crowd's lived encounters.

Development and Development:

Dynamic characters, the individuals who go through critical change or development all through the story, will quite often leave an enduring effect.

The excursion of a person, set apart by difficulties, mishaps, and self-disclosure, reflects the human experience. The course of advancement permits crowds to observe the person's improvement as well as reflects parts of their very own development.

An excellent illustration of character development is Ebenezer Penny pincher in Charles Dickens' "A holiday song." From a tightfisted and unfeeling individual, Tightwad changes into an empathetic and liberal soul through experiences with phantoms and reflections on his past. This change reverberates on the grounds that it represents the limit with respect to change and reclamation inside each person.

True Exchange and Voice:

Characters wake up through their exchange and one of a kind voices. Bona fide and all around created exchange progresses the plot as well as uncovers features of the's characters, connections, and clashes. Each character ought to have a particular voice that mirrors their experience, character, and encounters.

Consider the unmistakable exchange of Imprint Twain's Huckle-berry Finn, mirroring the vernacular of the time and area. This realness improves the person's trustworthiness as well as drenches perusers in the social setting of the story. Voice goes past simple words; it includes the musicality, tone, and characteristics that make characters essential.

Defective Authenticity:

Wonderful characters can be forgettable; imperfect characters are frequently the most significant. Blemishes make characters interesting, human, and powerless to similar difficulties and missteps as the crowd. The imperfections of a person add to their validness and set out open doors for development and recovery.

Perhaps of writing's most notorious person, Hamlet, is loaded with imperfections — delay, hesitation, and an inclination for self-question. These defects make Hamlet a profoundly human person, permitting crowds to sympathize with his unseen conflicts and existential inquiries. Imperfect authenticity adds profundity as well as gives a mirror to the crowd to consider their own weaknesses.

Powerful Utilization of Origin story:

A person's history, when decisively uncovered, can add layers of profundity and close to home reverberation. Whether through flashbacks, recollections, or continuous disclosures, the history shapes the person's present and impacts their inspirations. Histories offer a brief look into a person's previous injuries, delights, and vital minutes that formed who they have become.

Darth Vader from the "Star Wars" adventure is a perfect representation of a person whose history significantly influences the story.

The disclosure of Anakin Skywalker's tumble to the clouded side and change into Darth Vader adds intricacy to the person, evoking both sympathy and dread. Really meshing origin story into the account enhances the person's excursion and gives crowds a more far reaching comprehension of their inspirations.

Vital Bad guys:

The effect of a story frequently relies on the strength of its main bad guy. A convincing bad guy isn't just a foil for the hero yet a person with inspirations, profundity, and a remarkable viewpoint. A noteworthy bad guy difficulties the hero in manners that go past actual showdown, constraining them to face their own convictions, shortcomings, or moral limits.

The personality of Hannibal Lecter in Thomas Harris' "The Quiet of the Sheep" is a great representation of a vital bad guy. Lecter's insight, refinement, and complex brain research lift him past a customary reprobate. A very much created bad guy adds pressure, intricacy, and moral uncertainty to the story, having an enduring impact on the crowd.

Social and Social Pertinence:

Characters that resound with crowds frequently mirror the social and social settings in which they exist. By tending to pertinent subjects and issues, characters become a focal point through which crowds investigate and draw in with more extensive cultural worries. Characters can challenge generalizations, feature social shameful acts, or act as images of flexibility and trust.

The personality of Atticus Finch in Harper Lee's "To Kill a Mockingbird" typifies social and social importance. As a principled legal counselor shielding an honest Person of color in a racially charged Southern town, Atticus turns into an image of moral uprightness and the battle against foul play. Characters that resound in a social and social setting have the ability to rouse reflection and add to more extensive discussions.

1. **Eccentric Personalities**

   Unusual characters add a lively and frequently eccentric aspect to the embroidery of human cooperations. Embracing uniqueness and shunning similarity, people with whimsical characters oppose cultural standards and challenge regular assumptions. Whether celebrated, misjudged, or excused, these whimsical characters add to the variety of human experience, making a permanent imprint on the social scene.

   Characterizing Unpredictability:

   Unpredictability is a diverse idea that rises above a simple deviation from normal practices. It incorporates an unmistakable and eccentric way to deal with life, frequently described by offbeat way of behaving, interests, or standpoints.

   Unusual people might show characteristics, impossible to miss propensities, or eccentric styles of articulation that put them aside from the standard.

   Essentially, unpredictability isn't inseparable from pathology or brokenness. While a few erratic people might show qualities related with psychological wellness conditions, many basically have a free thinker soul that appears in their ways of life, interests, and connections.

   Social Symbols and Flightiness:

Social history is packed with notorious figures whose erraticisms have raised them to amazing status. Consider Salvador Dalí, the surrealist painter known for his showy mustache, abnormal style sense, and strange workmanship. Dalí's unconventionality reached out past his canvases, pervading his whole persona and laying out him as an image of creative individuality.

Another eminent model is Frida Kahlo, the Mexican painter prestigious for her self-representations and proud hug of her novel character. From her unmistakable unibrow to her dynamic Tehuana dresses, Kahlo's capriciousness was not restricted to her imaginative undertakings however saturated each part of her life.

Scholarly Unusualness:

Unpredictability frequently tracks down articulation in scholarly pursuits, with unusual masterminds testing laid out standards and reshaping how we might interpret the world. Nikola Tesla, the spearheading innovator and physicist, is a quintessential illustration of a mentally unusual person. Tesla's unconventional thoughts and visionary ideas, like remote transmission of energy, were somewhat radical and frequently considered erratic during his period.

Likewise, Buckminster Fuller, the visionary draftsman, creator, and futurist, was known for his whimsical way to deal with plan and his obligation to making answers for worldwide difficulties. Fuller's geodesic vaults, which tried to change lodging, were significant of his imaginative and erratic vision for a more economical future.

Erraticism in Writing:

The domain of writing is abounding with characters whose whimsies make them important and charming. In Lewis Carroll's "Alice's Experiences in Wonderland," the Distraught Hatter and the Cheshire Feline stand as perfect representations of whimsical characters. The Frantic Hatter's interminable casual get-together and the Cheshire Feline's confounding grin make no sense and add to the capricious and dreamlike air of Wonderland.

In J.K. Rowling's "Harry Potter" series, Albus Dumbledore, the unusual head administrator of Hogwarts School of Black magic and Wizardry, typifies scholarly erraticism. Dumbledore's unpredictable way to deal with initiative, his propensity for enigmatic comments, and his irregular decisions put him aside as a person whose erraticism is indispensable to his insight and intricacy.

Difficulties of Erraticism:

While erraticism can be commended for its commitments to inventiveness and advancement, capricious people frequently face difficulties and cultural investigation. Resistance can be met with suspicion, and the people who digress from laid out standards might be seen as problematic or flighty to the place of unusualness. Unusualness can prompt social disengagement or underestimation, with people confronting opposition or misconception from the individuals who stick all the more near cultural shows.

Moreover, capriciousness might be seen through a social or verifiable focal point, with ways of behaving that are viewed as unpredictable in one period or setting being acknowledged or even celebrated in another. This ease features the abstract idea of whimsy and the significance of social setting in understanding and valuing unpredictable ways of behaving.

Unconventionality as a Wellspring of Imagination:

Unconventional people frequently station their extraordinary points of view into imaginative pursuits, adding to headways in artistic expression, sciences, and different fields. The capacity to think outside customary limits, combined with an eagerness to embrace eccentric thoughts, can prompt pivotal developments and imaginative magnum opuses.

Steve Occupations, prime supporter of Macintosh Inc., is an outstanding illustration of a visionary with unconventional propensities. Occupations' irregular administration style, accentuation on plan feel, and obligation to pushing innovative limits were indispensable to Apple's prosperity. His whimsies, while trying for everyone around him, assumed a huge part in cultivating a culture of development.

Exploring Unconventionality in Regular daily existence:

For people with unconventional characters exploring regular daily existence, finding a harmony among legitimacy and cultural assumptions can be a fragile dance. Embracing one's whimsies can prompt a more extravagant, really satisfying life, yet it might likewise involve a level of flexibility despite cultural standards.

Effective route of capriciousness frequently includes finding strong networks that value variety and encourage individual articulation. Imagination and advancement flourish in conditions that commend dissention, and people with offbeat propensities might track down comfort and consolation in spaces that esteem their extraordinary viewpoints.

Embracing Unconventionality:

Society stands to profit from embracing unconventionality as opposed to pathologizing or defaming it. The variety of thought, thoughts, and viewpoints that flighty people offer of real value can fuel development, rock the boat, and add to a more unique and comprehensive culture.

Establishing conditions that energize credibility, celebrate variety, and oblige a scope of articulations can encourage a climate where erraticism isn't just acknowledged yet in addition esteemed. By recognizing the positive commitments of unpredictable people, society can move past tight meanings of business as usual and embrace the lavishness that accompanies embracing different perspectives and being.

2. **Comedic Archetypes**

Comedic models, established in the immortal practice of humor, act as comfortable layouts that reverberate with crowds across societies and ages. These originals, described by particular qualities and circumstances, give a system to the making of comedic characters and stories. From the blundering blockhead to the clever joke artist, comedic paradigms add to the comprehensiveness of chuckling and the persevering through allure of humor.

The Blundering Nitwit:

The blundering fool is an exemplary comedic model described by their absence of insight, ungainliness, and frequently benevolent yet misinformed activities. This model inspires giggling through a blend of actual satire, misconceptions, and the comedic results of their clumsiness. From Charlie Chaplin's notorious depiction of the Vagrant to Mr. Bean's quiet misfortunes, the blundering fool is an all inclusive figure that rises above language obstructions.

The humor got from the blundering fool prime example frequently emerges from the crowd's capacity to perceive and identify with the person's imperfections. Whether they are exploring social circumstances, endeavoring basic errands, or participating in droll humor, the blundering moron's jokes give a comedic reflect mirroring the ridiculousness of human imprudence.

The Straight Man and Comic Pair:

The unique transaction between the straight man and the comic pair is an exemplary comedic original that depends on the differentiation between two characters. The straight man is the more serious, judicious, and frequently exasperated individual, while the comic pair accomplice is whimsical, eccentric, and inclined to comedic trickeries.

Abbott and Costello, Tree and Solid, and Key and Peele are instances of comedic pairs that have dominated this original. The comedic strain emerges from the straight man's endeavors to explore the turbulent world made by their capricious partner. This paradigm blossoms with the science between the two characters, making a comedic collaboration that elevates the humor and draws in the crowd in the exchange of differentiating characters.

The Clever Comedian:

The clever comedian is a shrewd and frequently naughty person who explores the comedic scene with tricky and wit.

This original depends on mind, smart chat, and a talent for out-maneuvering others. Whether it's Shakespeare's Puck, Bugs Rabbit, or the prankster figures found in different folklores, this model savors the experience of making turmoil and disarray through their fast reasoning and shrewd plans.

The humor in the clever prankster paradigm frequently rises out of their capacity to reverse the situation on power figures, challenge cultural standards, and use language as a device for disruption. The joke artist's shenanigans feature the idiocies of rules and shows, welcoming the crowd to delight in the delight of scholarly perkiness.

The Humorous Social Pundit:

The mocking social pundit is a comedic model that uses humor as a focal point to scrutinize and ridicule cultural standards, organizations, and shows. This model frequently shows up as a sharp-witted reporter, uncovering bad faith, silliness, and the eccentricities of human way of behaving. Jon Stewart's job as the host of "The Day to day Show" and George Carlin's stand-up schedules represent this prime example, as they use humor to take apart and parody contemporary issues.

The ironical social pundit's humor is established in observational satire and a sharp familiarity with cultural subtleties. By featuring the inconsistencies and idiocies present in regular daily existence, this prime example welcomes the crowd to ponder the human condition while giving a soothing delivery through chuckling.

The Stupid Power Figure:

The stupid power figure is a comedic prime example that plays on the confusion between a person's, important, influential place and their absence of capability or intelligence. This paradigm undermines customary thoughts of power, depicting pioneers, supervisors, or figures of power as humorously bumbling. Whether it's Controller Clouseau from the "Pink Puma" series or Michael Scott from "The Workplace," the stupid power figure inspires giggling through their off track choices and negligence.

The humor in this model frequently comes from the crowd's acknowledgment of the idiocy intrinsic in the people who stand firm on footholds of power yet miss the mark on important abilities or judgment. The stupid power figure turns into a wellspring of comedic incongruity, testing assumptions about initiative and order.

The Loveable Maverick:

The loveable rebel is a magnetic and frequently ethically equivocal person who explores the comedic scene with appeal, dauntlessness, and a propensity for naughtiness. Han Solo from "Star Wars," Jack Sparrow from "Privateers of the Caribbean," and Ferris Bueller are instances of the loveable rebel prime example. These characters catch the crowd's love through their crafty appeal, clever jokes, and capacity to explore difficulties with style.

The humor in the loveable maverick paradigm emerges from their capacity to challenge authority, beguile right in the clear, and keep a charming emanation notwithstanding their blemishes. This prime example frequently obscures the lines among good and bad, welcoming the crowd to pull for a person whose insubordinate soul challenges cultural standards.

2.2 Crafting Hilarious Dialogue

Making diverting discourse is a craftsmanship that consolidates mind, timing, and a comprehension of character elements. Whether in writing, film, or theater, the capacity to make discourse that evokes chuckling depends on the transaction of language, humor gadgets, and a sharp consciousness of comedic timing. As characters participate in entertaining chitchat, clever repartee, or ridiculous trades, the exchange turns into a vehicle for humor that reverberates with crowds.

Understanding Person Voice:

Successful comedic discourse starts with a profound comprehension of each character's exceptional voice. Each character brings an unmistakable character, viewpoint, and set of eccentricities to the discussion.

Whether it's the mocking tone of a savvy companion, the empty conveyance of an emotionless person, or the rich excitement of a capricious character, the person's voice makes way for comedic connections.

The subtleties of character voice incorporate the words expressed as well as the musicality, pacing, and mannerisms of discourse. The juxtaposition of differentiating voices inside a discourse, for example, matching a verbose person with a brisk one, improves comedic potential. By remaining consistent with each character's voice, journalists make a genuine and clever exchange that feels natural to the account.

Utilizing Humor Gadgets:

Humor gadgets are fundamental apparatuses in creating diverting exchange. These gadgets incorporate pleasantry, plays on words, risqué remark, incongruity, and misrepresentation, among others. The essential utilization of these gadgets adds layers of comedic profundity to the exchange, permitting characters to play with language in unforeseen and entertaining ways.

Wit, like quips and shrewd manners of speaking, infuses an energetic component into the exchange. It welcomes the crowd to draw in with language on different levels, appreciating the keenness and mind implanted in the words expressed. For example, Oscar Wilde was an expert of pleasantry, and his plays like "The Significance of Being Sincere" grandstand the comedic force of semantic gymnastics.

Incongruity, whether situational or verbal, makes humor by undermining assumptions. Characters saying one thing while at the same time meaning one more or ending up in ludicrous circumstances add to the great flightiness of comedic exchange. This component of shock connects with the crowd and keeps them honest, expecting the following turn or zinger.

Misrepresentation is one more impressive humor gadget that intensifies the ludicrousness of exchange. Characters who hyperbolize circumstances, feelings, or qualities infuse a portion of comicalness into the discussion. This comedic distortion resounds with crowds since it amplifies conspicuous parts of human way of behaving to amusing limits.

Dominating Timing and Musicality:

Comedic timing is a vital part of making entertaining discourse. The pacing and musicality of the discussion direct when zingers land, when stops make expectation, and when the rhythm advances for comedic impact. A very much coordinated conveyance upgrades the effect of jokes and permits the crowd to relish the humor.

Consider the quick fire trades in exemplary screwball comedies like "His Young lady Friday," where characters participate in clever and excited chat. The speedy beat of the discourse, combined with exact stops for zingers, adds to the comedic brightness of the scenes. Timing isn't just about conveying lines; it's tied in with arranging the rhythmic movement of the discourse to expand comedic influence.

Investigating Disjointedness and Ludicrousness:

Disjointedness and ludicrousness are powerful components in creating funny discourse. Putting characters in unforeseen or mixed up circumstances makes fruitful ground for humor. Whether it's a proper setting disturbed by flippant language or characters responding ludicrously to everyday circumstances, disjointedness produces comedic pressure and shock.

The sitcom "Seinfeld" magnificently used ambiguity by investigating the humor in regular circumstances. The characters' talk about trivial issues, combined with their overstated responses to apparently unimportant occasions, featured the ludicrousness of human way of behaving. By amplifying the disjointed qualities inborn in common life, the exchange turned into a steady wellspring of giggling.

Building Running Gags and Callbacks:

Running gags and callbacks are viable procedures for supporting humor all through a story. By presenting repeating components, expressions, or jokes, essayists make a feeling of coherence that gathers comedic speed. Running gags give a string of commonality that resounds with crowds, inspiring giggling through the acknowledgment of repeating themes.

The TV series "Captured Improvement" is famous for its many-sided snare of running gags and callbacks. Characters reference previous occasions, rehash expressions, and participate in repeating ways of behaving that become comedic themes all through the series. The result comes while these running gags develop and converge, making layers of humor for committed watchers.

Taking into account Impromptu creation and Immediacy:

Now and again, the sorcery of comedic discourse lies in the immediacy of ad lib. While prearranged exchange frames the establishment, passing on space for entertainers to ad lib considers certifiable, in-the-second humor to arise. Spontaneous creation adds a component of eccentricism and legitimacy to the exchange, cultivating a unique interchange between entertainers.

The movies of chief Judd Apatow, for example, "Telecaster" and "Superbad," frequently integrate improvisational components. Entertainers are urged to investigate their characters and contribute unconstrained lines, bringing about exchange that feels regular and unscripted. This cooperative way to deal with making discourse upgrades the comedic science among entertainers and makes snapshots of startling cleverness.

Adjusting Nuance and Obviousness:

Making diverting exchange includes a fragile harmony among nuance and obviousness. While some humor blossoms with shrewd pleasantry and nuanced perceptions, other comedic minutes benefit from a more straightforward and obvious methodology. Journalists should measure the tone of the story and the characters required to figure out some kind of harmony between inconspicuous mind and strong humor.

In the TV series "The Workplace," the mockumentary design considers unpretentious and nuanced comedic minutes through character articulations and uncomfortable silences. All the while, the obvious, direct-to-camera interviews give chances to characters to offer their internal viewpoints and convey zingers with a more unequivocal comedic influence.

1. **Wordplay and Puns**

   Pleasantry and quips, frequently viewed as etymological tumbling, infuse humor and perkiness into language by taking advantage of the various implications and hints of words. These smart etymological gadgets add a layer of mind to different types of correspondence, from writing and jokes to promoting and regular discussions. Wit, portrayed by its flexibility and capacity to evoke chuckling through phonetic shrewdness, has turned into a valued part of human articulation.

   Characterizing Wit:

   Wit includes an expansive range of etymological gadgets that exploit the various implications, sounds, or designs of words to make humor, equivocalness, or smart associations. It can appear in different structures, including plays on words, risqué remark, re-arranged words, homophones, and other cunning controls of language. The quintessence of wit lies in the delight of language investigation, where words become devices for entertainment and scholarly commitment.

   Jokes as a Quintessential Pleasantry:

   At the core of pleasantry, jokes stand apart as a quintessential and frequently misjudged type of semantic humor. A quip includes a pun that have various implications or comparable sounds, making a silly and at times moan commendable impact. Quips can work at different levels, from basic plays on homophones to additional complex semantic turns.

   For example, the exemplary joke "Time passes quickly like a bolt; organic product flies like a banana" features the double implications of "flies," showing how quips energetically exploit language ambiguities. Quips are semantic vaulting as well as mental riddles that draw in the psyche in unraveling numerous layers of significance inside a solitary expression.

Abstract Wit:

In writing, wit fills in as a useful asset for essayists to mix humor, keenness, and scholarly profundity into their works. Creators frequently use jokes, risqué statement, and different types of wit to make vital characters, clever exchange, and shrewd unexpected developments. Shakespeare, prestigious for his etymological ability, utilized wit widely in his plays and works.

In "Hamlet," Shakespeare releases a fountain of quips, twofold implications, and shrewd wit. The renowned line "Regarding life, what to think about it, that is the issue" investigates existential subjects as well as exploits the rehashed utilization of the action word "to be" for etymological impact. The wit in Shakespeare's works rises above language obstructions, showing the immortal allure of smart control of words.

Promoting and Trademarks:

Pleasantry is a pervasive component in publicizing and marking, where snappy mottos and important expressions frequently depend on etymological cunning to have an enduring effect. A very much created joke or statement with a double meaning can improve brand review and make the publicizing message really captivating. Sponsors influence pleasantry to make vital slogans that catch consideration and convey the substance of an item or administration.

For instance, the cheap food chain McDonald's begat the renowned trademark "I'm lovin' it," which conveys a positive feeling as well as utilizes the everyday "lovin'" as a play on "cherishing." This straightforward yet viable wit adds to the motto's memorability and social effect.

Ordinary Discussions:

In ordinary discussions, pleasantry adds a dash of humor and levity to collaborations. Individuals frequently participate in jokes, clever comments, or sharp manners of speaking to entertain others and make a carefree air. Wit turns into a common phonetic jungle gym where people can exhibit their inventiveness, knowledge, and comical inclination.

Easygoing wit can go from basic quips because of a recognizable expression to additional intricate etymological games. Companions bantering, associates trading clever comments, and relatives taking part in energetic verbal trades all add to the lavishness of language in friendly settings.

Social and Culturally diverse Wit:

Pleasantry is profoundly implanted in social articulations, expressions, and etymological customs. Various societies display exceptional types of wit that mirror their semantic subtleties and verifiable settings. Diverse correspondence frequently includes exploring etymological humor, where understanding pleasantry becomes urgent for valuing the nuances of jokes and articulations.

For example, Chinese language and culture are wealthy in semantic wit, including jokes, homophones, and character-based humor. The utilization of homophones in Chinese considers jokes and pleasantry that may not be straightforwardly translatable however add layers of importance and entertainment for local speakers.

Difficulties and Ambiguities:

While wit is a wellspring of phonetic joy, it likewise presents difficulties, particularly in interpretation and culturally diverse correspondence. Jokes and pleasantry frequently depend on the particular sounds or designs of a specific language, making direct interpretation troublesome. The social and etymological setting where wit emerges can likewise add to vagueness, as translations might fluctuate in light of individual points of view and knowledge of colloquial articulations.

Furthermore, not all crowds might appreciate or decipher pleasantry similarly. Some might delight in the keenness of phonetic gymnastics, while others might find specific types of wit befuddling or in any event, disturbing. Finding some kind of harmony among mind and openness is a thought for makers utilizing wit in different settings.

2. **Timing and Delivery**

Timing and conveyance are basic components in the specialty of humor, molding the adequacy of comedic minutes in different types of diversion, from stand-up satire and sitcoms to movies and writing.

The nuanced exchange between when a joke is conveyed and what it is introduced essentially impacts its mean for on the crowd. The authority of timing and conveyance requires a comprehension of comedic mood, expectation, and the wise utilization of stops, guaranteeing that the zinger lands with most extreme impact.

Comedic Mood and Pacing:

At the center of timing and conveyance is the idea of comedic mood. Comedic mood includes the intentional game plan of words, expressions, or activities to make an example that draws in the crowd and constructs expectation. Laying out a cadenced stream permits jokesters, entertainers, or journalists to explore through arrangements and zingers with accuracy.

In stand-up parody, for instance, a humorist's conveyance is in many cases described by an unmistakable beat that directs the crowd through the comedic venture. The planning of stops, the rhythm of discourse, and the intentional pacing of jokes add to the generally speaking comedic musicality. A deep rooted mood not just upgrades the comedic effect of individual lines yet additionally makes a feeling of union and congruity in the exhibition.

Expectation and Shock:

Timing and conveyance blossom with the fragile harmony among expectation and shock. Expectation makes way for a zinger by making an assumption inside the crowd. Gifted entertainers utilize this expectation for their potential benefit, driving the crowd down a recognizable way prior to undermining assumptions with an unforeseen turn.

The component of shock, when all around coordinated, upgrades the comedic impact. Whether it's an unexpected change in tone, an unforeseen zinger, or a wind in the story, astonishing the crowd at the right second creates chuckling by surprising them. The exchange among expectation and shock depends on a sharp consciousness of the crowd's assumptions and the capacity to undermine those assumptions with comedic artfulness.

The Force of Stops:

The essential utilization of stops is a sign of successful timing and conveyance in satire. Stops act as accentuation marks, permitting the crowd to ingest data, process the arrangement, and expect the zinger. The term and position of stops can fundamentally impact the comedic effect of a line or execution.

In stand-up parody, comics frequently utilize very much coordinated stops to fabricate strain prior to conveying a zinger. The pregnant respite makes a snapshot of tension, increasing the crowd's expectation and making way for a hilarious disclosure. Essentially, in sitcoms or movies, entertainers influence stops to permit the crowd to enlist the humor in a line or a circumstance, enhancing the comedic impact.

Actual Timing in Visual Satire:

In visual parody, for example, droll or actual humor, timing stretches out past verbal conveyance to envelop actual activities and signals. The execution of comedic tricks, flummoxes, or visual gags requires flawless timing to boost giggling. Actual timing includes definitively arranging developments, responses, and visual components to synchronize with the generally comedic beat.

Think about the exemplary actual satire of Charlie Chaplin or Buster Keaton. Their dominance of actual timing, communicated through exact developments and looks, raised quiet film parody to a work of art. The synchronization of activities with comedic beats and the cautious coordination of visual components added to the getting through allure of their work.

Social Contemplations:

Timing and conveyance are additionally affected by social subtleties and the setting in which satire is introduced. Various societies might have unmistakable comedic rhythms, inclinations for timing, and assumptions about the speed of humor. Humorists and makers should be sensitive to the social setting in which their work is gotten to guarantee that timing resounds with the target group.

For instance, the planning of jokes in Japanese stand-up satire, known as "manzai," depends on a particular musicality including a high speed trade between two entertainers. Understanding and adjusting to social varieties in comedic timing is critical for making humor that rises above phonetic and social boundaries.

Assortment in Timing Styles:

Timing and conveyance in parody envelop a range of styles, considering flexibility in connecting with crowds. A few humorists or comedic exhibitions might flourish with fast fire conveyance, with jokes conveyed with hardly a pause in between to keep a high-energy pace. This style is frequently connected with professional comics like Robin Williams or Eddie Murphy, who enrapture crowds with their dynamic and high speed conveyance.

On the other hand, other comedic styles might embrace a more intentional and estimated way to deal with timing. Lifeless humor, portrayed by downplayed conveyance and negligible articulation, depends on the planning of unpretentious subtleties to inspire giggling. Jokesters like Steven Wright or dry-witted characters, for example, Ron Swanson from "Parks and Diversion" exhibit the adequacy of slow, conscious timing in making comedic influence.

Adjusting to Mediums:

Compelling timing and conveyance likewise include adjusting to the particular mechanism of articulation. Professional comics, for example, participate in an immediate and close relationship with the crowd, requiring an intense consciousness of live responses and reactions. Conversely, comedic entertainers in movie or TV should consider the pacing of scenes, the planning of alters, and the cooperative elements with individual cast individuals and chiefs.

The change from stage to screen requires a nuanced comprehension of how timing deciphers in various settings. Jokesters who effectively explore both live exhibitions and on-screen jobs, like Richard Pryor or Joan Streams, show the flexibility expected to adjust comedic timing to different mediums.

3 |

Chapter 3

Plotting for Laughs

Plotting for snickers is a nuanced try that includes creating comedic stories, character curves, and situational humor to evoke giggling from the crowd. Whether in writing, film, or TV, the craft of comedic plotting requires a sharp comprehension of comedic timing, character elements, and the components that drive humor. Fruitful comedic plots frequently include a blend of shrewd arrangements, surprising turns, and interesting circumstances that resound with the crowd's funny bone.

Laying out a Comedic Reason:

At the core of plotting for giggles is the foundation of a comedic premise that fills in as the establishment for the story. The reason makes way for the humor that will unfurl, presenting components, characters, or circumstances that innately loan themselves to comedic potential. The reason frequently includes misrepresentation, incoherency, or the disruption of assumptions, making a ripe ground for humor to thrive.

Think about the reason of the TV series "The Workplace," which spins around the everyday and frequently silly elements of an office work environment. The comedic potential emerges from the appeal of work environment situations joined with the overstated peculiarities of the characters. Laying out areas of strength for a reason permits makers to construct a structure that reliably produces humor all through the story.

Character-driven Humor:

In comedic plotting, characters assume a focal part in driving humor. Advanced characters with particular characters, characteristics, and blemishes become channels for comedic circumstances and collaborations. The juxtaposition of differentiating characters, each with their interesting comedic ascribes, improves the general humor of the plot.

Character-driven humor frequently includes taking advantage of the quirks and weaknesses of people inside the account. These idiosyncrasies might go from misrepresented character qualities to exceptional propensities, giving a wellspring of comedic material. The sitcom "Companions," for instance, gets humor from the unmistakable characters of its characters, like Joey's dimwitted appeal or Ross' psychotic inclinations.

Sharp Arrangements and Adjustments:

Comedic plotting depends on the essential utilization of arrangements and adjustments to expand chuckling. Smart arrangements lay out the basis for a comedic circumstance or joke, making expectation inside the crowd. The result, frequently conveyed through unforeseen turns, uncovers, or zingers, profits by this expectation to produce giggling.

The exemplary comedic gadget of the arrangement and result is exemplified in the film "Groundhog Day." The reason of a man remembering that very day more than once sets up various comedic situations. Every reiteration constructs expectation, and the settlements emerge from the hero's advancing responses and endeavors to explore the craziness of the circumstance.

Disjointedness and Confusion:

Disjointedness, the condition awkward or conflicting, is an integral asset in comedic plotting. Causing circumstances where components conflict or go amiss from assumptions produces humor through the acknowledgment of the ludicrous or startling. Confusion, a type of disjointedness, includes driving the crowd in one heading before suddenly moving to another, surprising them for comedic impact.

The movie "Plane!" wonderfully utilizes ambiguity and confusion. Set inside the serious setting of a fiasco film, the film presents silly and incomprehensible components, like over-the-top discourse and strange visual gags. The confusion lies in the unforeseen humor inside a generally serious type, making a comedic balance that resounds with crowds.

Acceleration of Ridiculousness:

Comedic plots frequently blossom with the acceleration of ludicrousness, where each progressive occasion or disclosure turns out to be more extraordinary than the last. This heightening gathers comedic speed, leaving the crowd in a condition of ceaseless shock and entertainment. The key is to push the limits of the account's craziness while keeping up with interior consistency.

The enlivened series "Rick and Morty" is a great representation of the heightening of craziness. The show, revolved around the unpredictable researcher Rick and his grandson Morty, reliably increase the craziness of its science fiction situations, making a dreamlike and hilarious story. The heightening turns into a characterizing highlight, welcoming crowds to embrace the flightiness and idiocy of the show's universe.

Undermining Sayings and Shows:

Plotting for snickers frequently includes undermining customary figures of speech and account shows. By taking recognizable story components and flipping them completely around, makers present oddity and shock, making a comedic influence. Disruption can happen at the degree of type, character bends, or even the goal of the plot.

The film "Shaun of the Dead" keenly undermines the zombie class by imbuing it with humor and sarcastic components. Rather than sticking to customary frightfulness shows, the film compares zombie end of the world situations with ordinary humor, making an interesting and comedic take on the class.

Equal Storylines and Intertwined Plots:

Integrating equal storylines or interlaced plots adds intricacy and profundity to comedic accounts. Numerous plotlines can combine surprisingly, making comedic impacts and cooperative energies. The interaction between various characters and their singular circular segments improves the generally comedic experience, giving a dynamic and layered story.

The TV series "Captured Improvement" succeeds in joined plots, with each character seeking after their comedic goals that in the end cross. The intricacy of the account, loaded up with callbacks, running gags, and covering storylines, adds to the show's comedic extravagance and prizes mindful watchers.

Timing and Pacing:

The effective execution of comedic plotting depends on exact timing and pacing. Comedic beats should be arranged with artfulness, permitting the crowd to ingest data, expect zingers, and appreciate the humor. The mood of the plot, much the same as comedic timing in execution, directs the crowd through the story's comedic venture.

Think about the film "Bridesmaids," which amazingly balances comedic timing and pacing. The plot unfurls with a progression of raising comedic circumstances, each carefully coordinated for most extreme effect. The film's pacing considers the slow advancement of humor, guaranteeing that every scene adds to the in general comedic energy.

Social and Social Critique:

Integrating social and social critique inside comedic plots adds layers of importance and significance. Ironical components or entertaining perceptions about cultural standards, patterns, or shows give an extra aspect to the humor. Comedic accounts that reverberate with the crowd's social setting improve the appeal of the plot.

The enlivened series "South Park" embodies the reconciliation of social and social discourse into comedic plotting. The show utilizes parody to address recent developments, cultural issues, and mainstream society, implanting humor with a basic focal point. By mixing satire with discourse, "South Park" stays an important and significant comedic force.

3.1 Building Comic Tension

Building comic pressure is a fragile workmanship that includes making a feeling of expectation, shock, and delivery inside the crowd, finishing in chuckling. This talented control of pressure is a major part of comedic narrating, tracked down in different types of diversion, including stand-up parody, sitcoms, movies, and writing. Effectively constructing comic pressure requires a nuanced comprehension of comedic timing, character elements, and the components that incite giggling.

Laying out a Comedic Reason:

The underpinning of building comic strain lies in laying out a comedic premise that lays the foundation for silly circumstances. The reason makes way for the comedic story, presenting components, characters, or situations that innately have comedic potential. This underlying arrangement makes expectation inside the crowd, flagging that humor will emerge from the unfurling occasions.

In stand-up satire, the reason is many times laid out through the entertainer's initial lines or the focal topic of their daily practice. For instance, on the off chance that a jokester starts by examining the peculiarities of regular day to day existence or the idiocies of specific circumstances, they are laying the foundation for comic strain by flagging that the everyday will be changed into something diverting.

Shrewd Arrangements and Expectation:

Shrewd arrangements are indispensable to building comic strain. These arrangements include making situations or circumstances that lead the crowd in a particular course, making expectation for a comedic result. The essential utilization of language, timing, and situational components adds to the crowd's assumption, making way for the humor to unfurl.

Consider the exemplary comedic arrangement of a person endeavoring a commonplace undertaking with the assumption that all that will go without a hitch. The expectation works as the crowd perceives the potential for something to go divertingly amiss. Whether it's a person attempting to gather furniture or explore a straightforward social communication, the cunning arrangement makes preparations for the comedic strain that will be settled through surprising turns or zingers.

Character Elements and Connections:

In comedic narrating, character elements assume a critical part in building pressure. Clear cut characters with particular characters, peculiarities, and connections become vessels for humor. The exchange between characters, their differentiating qualities, and the potential for struggle or false impressions add to the development of comedic pressure.

The sitcom "Frasier" is an astounding instance of utilizing character elements for comic pressure. The central protagonist, Dr. Frasier Crane, a complex and scholarly therapist, communicates with his practical dad, making a dynamic ready for humor. The strain emerges from the conflict of their characters and the comedic potential inborn in their contrasting points of view on life.

Acceleration and Uplifting:

Building comic strain frequently includes the essential heightening of occasions, progressively expanding the stakes or ridiculousness of a circumstance. This heightening uplifts the expectation inside the crowd, prompting a more critical comedic result. The key is to present components that lift the pressure while keeping up with inside consistency inside the comedic universe.

In the film "Imbecilic and More idiotic," the comedic strain raises as the two heroes, Lloyd and Harry, become trapped in a progression of progressively ludicrous and unbelievable circumstances. The heightening, from basic mistaken assumptions to expound misfortunes, adds to the film's comedic brightness. Each new improvement uplifts the strain, making a total impact that upgrades the general humor.

Timing and Pacing:

Dominating comedic timing and pacing is fundamental for successfully fabricating and delivering strain. The musicality of the story, the pacing of exchange, and the essential utilization of stops all add to the in general comedic experience.

Very much coordinated minutes permit the strain to mount, making expectation, prior to conveying the zinger or settling the comedic circumstance.

In stand-up parody, humorists utilize exact timing to fabricate strain prior to conveying a zinger. The intentional pacing of words, combined with all around coordinated stops, permits the crowd to expect the clever goal. Additionally, in prearranged satire, the planning of discourse conveyance, responses, and the general mood of scenes add to the development and arrival of comic strain.

Undermining Assumptions:

A strong strategy in building comic pressure is undermining crowd assumptions. By driving the crowd down a natural way and afterward going suddenly, makers produce shock and humor. This disruption can happen at different levels, from unexpected developments to the conveyance of zingers, keeping the crowd drew in and entertained.

The sitcom "Brooklyn Nine" frequently utilizes the procedure of undermining assumptions in its comedic plotting. The show presents recognizable police procedural situations yet undermines them with unforeseen person responses or unusual goals. This capriciousness adds to the show's capacity to amaze and entertain its crowd constantly.

Utilization of Incongruity and Incident:

Incongruity and occurrence are powerful devices for building comic pressure, as they make surprising exciting bends in the road in the account. Incongruity includes a differentiation among appearance and reality, while occurrence includes startling associations or occasions. The two components present a component of shock that adds to the humor of a circumstance.

In writing, crafted by P.G. Wodehouse, especially the Jeeves and Wooster series, are astonishing in involving incongruity and happenstance for comic impact. The misfortunes of Bertie Wooster, frequently brought about by amusing false impressions or incidental events, add to the hilarious tumult of the narratives.

Reiteration and Callbacks:

Reiteration and callbacks are strategies that add to the development of comic strain by returning to components or jokes presented before in the account. By rehashing specific expressions, activities, or comedic themes, makers make a feeling of commonality that enhances the humor upon every repeat.

The TV series "Captured Improvement" is famous for its utilization of reiteration and callbacks. Running gags, repeating expressions, and rehashed visual themes add to the show's comedic lavishness. The crowd's experience with these components permits the makers to fabricate strain and expectation, realizing that the result will include a smart callback to a formerly settled comedic component.

Actual Parody and Visual Gags:

Integrating actual parody and visual gags is an intense method for building and delivery comic strain. Droll humor, flummoxes, and misrepresented actual developments can make expectation as the crowd anticipates a hilarious result. The fruitful execution of these components depends on exact timing and the cautious coordination of actual activities.

The quiet movies of Charlie Chaplin, for example, "Present day Times," grandstand the brightness of building comic strain through actual satire. Chaplin's careful movement of comedic developments, combined perfectly, makes an ensemble of chuckling as the crowd expects and partakes in the actual humor unfurling onscreen.

Social and Social Editorial:

Building comic pressure can be advanced by integrating social and social discourse. Sarcastic components or amusing perceptions about cultural standards, patterns, or shows give an extra layer to the strain. By mixing satire with a basic focal point, makers can draw in the crowd mentally while as yet conveying snickers.

The stand-up satire of George Carlin frequently elaborate social analysis, and his capacity to construct strain through shrewd perceptions about society added to the effect of his humor. By featuring idiocies or logical inconsistencies in the social scene, Carlin made strain that was delivered through giggling, provoking both entertainment and thought.

1. **The Element of Surprise**

   The component of shock remains as a foundation in the domain of parody, a unique power that evokes certifiable chuckling by opposing assumptions and presenting the unforeseen. Whether in stand-up exhibitions, sitcoms, movies, or writing, the talented utilization of shock implants comedic minutes with a newness and capriciousness that dazzles crowds. This capacity to surprise watchers, driving them down an unanticipated way, is a strong comedic device that depends on shrewd arrangements, disruption of standards, and the essential organization of unforeseen turns.

   Smart Arrangements and Expectation:

   The component of shock starts with smart arrangements that lay out a specific setting or assumption inside the story. These arrangements make an underpinning of expectation, directing the crowd along a natural direction. It is inside this structure of expectation that the component of shock works most really.

   In stand-up parody, joke artists frequently utilize astute arrangements in their schedules. The initial lines or situations acquaint a reason that appears with line up with normal encounters or discernments.

   As the crowd becomes drenched in the normal, the stage is set for the jokester to capably undermine those assumptions and convey an unforeseen zinger, inciting chuckling through the component of shock.

   Disruption of Standards and Assumptions:

The strength of shock in satire is intently attached to the disruption of standards and cultural assumptions. By taking laid out shows and flipping them completely around, entertainers and makers present oddity, newness, and a feeling of the unforeseen. This deviation from the standard fills in as an impetus for chuckling as crowds have a great time the disjointedness.

In sitcoms, this disruption frequently works out as inversion or job exchanging. Characters acting in manners in spite of their laid out characteristics or challenging cultural standards give chances to astonishing comedic minutes. For example, a normally serious person taking part in droll humor or an inversion of orientation jobs can surprise watchers, producing giggling through the unforeseen.

Exciting bends in the road in Plotlines:

In prearranged parody, shock appears through exciting bends in the road in plotlines. Unanticipated turns of events, surprising person activities, or abrupt disclosures present a component of unconventionality that fills comedic force. The workmanship lies in creating these turns consistently, guaranteeing they resound with the laid out tone while conveying the ideal comedic influence.

Think about the TV series "Brooklyn Nine," where surprising unexpected developments and character advancements are basic to the show's humor. The abrupt change in elements, startling coalitions, or unexpected outcomes of characters' activities add to the unexpected component, keeping the crowd connected with and entertained.

Zingers and Timing in Stand-up Satire:

In the realm of stand-up satire, zingers are the central places where shock is released with greatest effect. The zinger conveys a surprising goal to the arrangement, undermining the crowd's assumptions and bringing out chuckling. The authority of timing is urgent in guaranteeing that the amazement is divulged with accuracy, permitting the crowd to appreciate the surprising development.

The late comic Mitch Hedberg was an expert of shock in his conveyance. His jokes frequently followed an example where the arrangement laid out an everyday or engaging situation, and the zinger veered off in a surprising and unexpected direction. The component of shock in Hedberg's parody lay in the effortlessness of the arrangement, making the deviation even more unforeseen and funny.

Visual Gags and Actual Parody:

The component of shock tracks down a characteristic home in visual gags and actual satire. Droll humor, flummoxes, and misrepresented actual developments exploit the component of shock, as horrifying acts lead to comical results. The progress of visual gags lies in the cautious arrangement of shock components, guaranteeing they line up with the comedic tone.

Charlie Chaplin's quiet movies are notable instances of utilizing visual gags and actual parody to evoke shock and giggling. Chaplin's capacity to control the climate, participate in horrendous acts, and explore through silly circumstances displayed the immortal allure of shock in satire.

Risqué remark and Pleasantry:

The verbal domain of satire flourishes with the component of shock through risqué remark and wit. Sharp controls of language, quips, and phonetic turns present shock by taking advantage of the numerous implications or hints of words. These phonetic gymnastics connect with the crowd's mental cycles, making a wonderful snapshot of acknowledgment that prompts giggling.

In stand-up schedules or prearranged discourse, humorists decisively send pleasantry to surprise the crowd. An apparently clear assertion veers off in a strange direction as the double implications of words are uncovered. This play on language presents shock as well as adds a scholarly layer to the humor.

Parody and Social Analysis:

Shock works on a more profound level in parody when mixed with parody and social editorial. By introducing a silly interpretation of cultural issues or standards, makers present shock through the surprising juxtaposition of humor and scrutinize. Ironical components frequently surprise crowds, testing assumptions and inciting reflection.

The mocking brightness of "The Onion," a sarcastic news association, lies in its capacity to utilize shock to undermine customary news detailing. Titles that at first seem veritable veer off in strange directions, uncovering the mocking plan and making an entertaining editorial on genuine occasions.

Eccentric Person Activities:

In both prearranged satire and writing, the component of shock is outfit through the activities of characters. At the point when characters stray from anticipated that way of behaving or go with choices opposite should their laid out qualities, it infuses a component of flightiness. This unexpected element creates chuckling as well as adds intricacy to character elements.

The personality of Michael Scott in the sitcom "The Workplace" epitomizes the utilization of erratic activities for comedic impact. Michael's choices and ways of behaving reliably challenge working environment standards, amazing both the characters inside the show and the crowd. This eccentricism adds to the humor and getting through allure of the person.

Social References and In-jokes:

Shock can be entwined with social references and in-jokes to make humor that resounds with explicit crowds. At the point when makers consolidate unforeseen references or unpretentious gestures to social peculiarities, it adds an additional layer of treat for those in the loop. This kind of humor depends on shared information, making a feeling of fellowship with the crowd.

The energized series "The Simpsons" is prestigious for its

utilization of social references and in-jokes. Whether through fast visual gags, sharp pleasantry, or ironical critique on mainstream society, the show shocks crowds via flawlessly incorporating these components into its comedic texture.

2. Running Gags

Running gags, those common comedic themes or topics that wind through different episodes or portions of a presentation, address a nuanced and getting through feature of parody. Whether utilized in stand-up schedules, TV programs, movies, or writing, running gags add to the improvement of an extraordinary comedic personality, cultivating a feeling of commonality and entertainment inside the crowd. The specialty of making and supporting running gags includes a fragile equilibrium of redundancy, innovativeness, and the capacity to develop these comedic components after some time.

Laying out the Establishment:

Running gags frequently find their underlying foundations in shrewd arrangements that present a common component or topic right on time in a comedic execution or story. These underlying presentations lay the preparation for future callbacks, making an expectant climate inside the crowd. The viability of running gags depends on the foundation of an establishment that is both noteworthy and versatile.

In stand-up satire, a humorist might present a running gag through a story, an expression, or a repetitive person. This underlying arrangement fills in as a comedic seed that, when returned to or developed, develops into a running gag that resounds with the crowd's memory and assumption.

Reiteration and Callbacks:

The heartbeat of running gags lies in reiteration and callbacks. The deliberate returning to of a particular comedic component makes a feeling of congruity and acknowledgment, encouraging a common encounter between the entertainer and the crowd. The redundancy turns into a phonetic or visual mark, engraving the running gag into the comedic personality of the exhibition.

In TV, running gags blossom with the force of redundancy. An expression rehashed by a person, a repetitive prop, or a particular visual theme turns into a string woven through various episodes. The redundancy welcomes crowds to expect these minutes, making a feeling of association and shared humor. The sitcom "Companions," for example, uses running gags like Ross' scandalous "We were on a break" line, which develops and repeats all through the series.

Advancement and Variety:

While reiteration is a key part, the life span of running gags frequently relies on their capacity to develop and adjust. The presentation of varieties or unforeseen turns keeps the comedic component from becoming flat. Running gags that show flexibility in their execution keep up with the crowd's advantage and lift the humor through shock.

In stand-up parody, a comic might present a running topic from the get-go in a daily practice and afterward play with varieties or unforeseen turns on that subject all through the exhibition. This versatility guarantees that the running gag stays crisp, giving the crowd new points to appreciate and snicker at the common component.

Character Consistency:

Running gags frequently revolve around predictable attributes or characteristics of characters, whether in sitcoms, movies, or writing. These qualities become comedic touchpoints that characterize the person's character and add to the general humor of the account. Consistency in character conduct, in any event, when overstated for comedic impact, builds up the running gag and improves its effect.

Think about the personality of Sheldon Cooper in the sitcom "The Theory of the universe's origin." His fixation on a particular spot on the love seat and his requirement for routine become running gags that reliably feature his peculiar nature. The unwavering quality of these attributes adds to the person's comedic allure and cultivates an association between the crowd and the common comedic components.

Social References and Meta-humor:

Running gags frequently rise above the quick comedic setting and integrate social references or meta-humor. By drawing on shared social information or making fun of the shows of the comedic structure itself, these gags make an extra layer of entertainment for keen crowds.

In writing, running gags might include meta-humor that recognizes the made up nature of the story. The "meta" viewpoint adds a mindfulness to the satire, welcoming perusers to draw in with the text on numerous levels. This can appear as characters breaking the fourth wall, recognizing the story design, or in any event, remarking on the ludicrousness of their own common jokes.

Inconspicuous Callbacks and Hidden little goodies:

Running gags can likewise appear as inconspicuous callbacks or Hidden little goodies, compensating mindful crowds with references to prior comedic minutes. These callbacks may not be plain yet act as a sign of approval for committed fans who value the congruity and interconnectedness of the comedic components.

In films, chiefs might incorporate unpretentious visual references or callbacks to running gags as a type of realistic Hidden goody. These unlikely treasures become a wellspring of joy for watchers who get these nuanced references, improving their pleasure in the generally comedic experience.

Timing and Pacing:

The adequacy of running gags is complicatedly attached to timing and pacing. All around coordinated redundancies and callbacks guarantee that the running gag lines up with the normal cadence of the comedic execution. The dividing between occurrences permits the crowd to see the value in the humor without it becoming repetitive.

In stand-up satire, the planning of returning to a running subject is urgent. Joke artists check crowd responses and decisively once again introduce the running gag at minutes that expand its comedic influence. This cautious arrangement of timing adds to the general progression of the exhibition.

Cohesiveness and Solidarity:

Running gags add to the cohesiveness and solidarity of a comedic execution or story. By stringing repeating components all through various sections or episodes, makers make a feeling of solidarity, permitting the crowd to interface with the overall comedic character. This solidarity changes running gags from disconnected jokes into essential parts of the comedic texture.

In TV series like "The Simpsons," running gags become a binding together power across episodes and seasons. The reliable presence of repeating components, whether characters, expressions, or visual gags, produces a feeling of cohesiveness that improves the show's persevering through notoriety.

Crowd Commitment and Association:

Running gags cultivate crowd commitment and association by laying out a continuous discourse among entertainers and watchers. The acknowledgment of a repetitive component makes a common encounter, manufacturing a connection between the comedic maker and the crowd. This association adds to the life span and effect of running gags, as they become piece of the aggregate comedic memory.

In live exhibitions, entertainers might measure crowd responses to running gags and adjust their conveyance in view of the crowd's reaction. This intelligent unique improves the association among entertainer and crowd, transforming running gags into shared comedic ceremonies.

3.2 Structuring a Comedic Plot

Organizing a comedic plot is a nuanced craftsmanship that includes creating a story structure intended to evoke chuckling and connect with the crowd's comical inclination. Whether in writing, film, or TV, effective comedic narrating depends on an essential plan of components, including shrewd arrangements, very much coordinated zingers, and the improvement of silly characters and circumstances. This mind boggling course of organizing a comedic plot includes cautious thought of pacing, heightening, and the exchange between different comedic gadgets.

Presentation and Laying out the Comedic Reason:

The start of a comedic plot is critical for setting the stage and laying out the comedic premise. This stage includes acquainting the crowd with the universe of the story and laying the preparation for the humor that will unfurl. The comedic premise fills in as the establishment, giving an unmistakable setting to the characters, circumstances, and clashes that will produce chuckling.

In writing, this presentation might include clever composition, comical exchange, or the introduction of a crazy circumstance that portends the comedic tone of the account. In film and TV, the initial scenes frequently present the focal comedic components, whether through visual gags, idiosyncratic characters, or clever circumstances, promptly indicating to the crowd that they are in for a comedic experience.

Character Presentation and Improvement:

Comedic plots blossom with advanced and appealing characters who become conductors for humor. The presentation of characters includes laying out their characters, idiosyncrasies, and inspirations in a way that lines up with the comedic tone of the story. These characters act as vehicles for humor, and their collaborations become key components in driving the comedic plot forward.

The advancement of silly characters might include misrepresenting specific qualities, making erratic characters, or setting them in crazy circumstances. The sitcom "Parks and Diversion," for instance, presents characters like Ron Swanson, whose lifeless conveyance and unemotional disposition add to the show's comedic lavishness. As the plot unfurls, the characters' characteristics become indispensable to producing chuckling.

Sharp Arrangements and Expectation:

Sharp arrangements are fundamental in organizing a comedic plot, as they make expectation and prepare for humor to unfurl. The arrangement presents components, situations, or clashes that intrinsically have comedic potential. These arrangements decisively guide the crowd's assumptions, making a feeling of expectation for the goal that will convey the comedic zinger.

In stand-up satire, the shrewd arrangement is the establishment for conveying a zinger that undermines or satisfies the crowd's assumptions. Jokesters magnificently use language, timing, and interesting situations to make arrangements that reverberate with the crowd's encounters, making way for the surprising turns that create giggling.

Struggle and Heightening of Humor:

Comedic plots frequently include clashes or difficulties that raise the humor, making a feeling of comedic force. The heightening of humor depends on a progressive expansion in ridiculousness, startling turns, or the strengthening of funny components. This acceleration keeps the crowd connected with and put resources into the unfurling comedic account.

Think about the film "Bridesmaids," where the contention rotates around the hero's misfortunes in wedding arranging. The humor heightens as the person's endeavors to explore social assumptions and individual difficulties become progressively silly. The acceleration heightens the comedic influence as well as adds to the general story curve.

All around coordinated Zingers and Goals:

The very much coordinated conveyance of zingers is a basic component in organizing a comedic plot. Zingers act as the result for sharp arrangements and raise the humor to its pinnacle. The planning of zingers is a craftsmanship in itself, requiring accuracy and an intense comprehension of comedic mood. Whether in writing, film, or stand-up satire, the fruitful execution of zingers is fundamental to evoking certifiable giggling.

In stand-up satire, the comic's conveyance of a zinger includes a blend of timing, tone, and frequently, a startling turn that surprises the crowd. In prearranged satire, the planning of exchange conveyance, visual gags, or situational goals adds to the viability of the zinger.

Disruption of Assumptions:

Organizing a comedic plot frequently includes the disruption of assumptions, where the story veers off in strange directions that oppose customary narrating. This disruption adds a component of shock to the humor, keeping the crowd connected with and entertained. By digressing from conventional plot directions, makers bring oddity and newness into the comedic experience.

The energized series "Rick and Morty" is known for its disruption of assumptions inside the science fiction classification. The show takes natural sayings and undermines them with startling unexpected developments, incorrigible humor, and capricious goals. This disruption adds to the show's one of a kind comedic character.

Intertwined Plots and Subplots:

Comedic plots can be improved by the intertwining of various plots and subplots, making intricacy and profundity. These interlaced accounts give potential open doors to comedic crashes, cooperative energies, and surprising associations. The elements between various characters and their singular curves add to the generally comedic experience.

The TV series "Captured Advancement" succeeds in entwined plots, where each character seeks after their comedic goals that in the long run converge. The intricacy of the account, loaded up with callbacks, running gags, and covering storylines, adds to the show's comedic wealth and prizes mindful watchers.

Social and Social Critique:

Implanting comedic plots with social and social editorial adds layers of significance and importance. Mocking components or clever perceptions about cultural standards, patterns, or shows give an extra aspect to the humor. Comedic accounts that reverberate with the crowd's social setting improve the appeal of the plot.

The mocking splendor of the energized series "South Park" lies in its joining of social and social analysis into comedic plotting. The show utilizes parody to address recent developments, cultural issues, and mainstream society, imbuing humor with a basic focal point. By mixing parody with critique, "South Park" stays a pertinent and significant comedic force.

Firm Goal and Conclusion:

Organizing a comedic plot requires a firm goal that integrates different components and gives conclusion to the crowd. The goal ought to line up with the comedic tone laid out all through the story, offering a wonderful end to the humor that has unfurled. Whether through a sharp curve, a callback to prior components, or a diverting disclosure, the goal adds to the general effect of the comedic experience.

In writing, the goal of a comedic plot might include the characters learning significant illustrations through comical misfortunes, prompting self-improvement and change. In film and TV, the last scenes frequently unite the different plot strings, furnishing a goal that resounds with the laid out comedic character.

1. **The Setup**

   At the core of each effective comedic try lies the craft of "The Arrangement." This fundamental component fills in as the establishment for creating chuckling, making ready for cunning zingers, unforeseen turns, and comedic gold. Whether in stand-up parody, sitcoms, movies, or writing, dominating the arrangement is a nuanced expertise that includes making expectation, drawing in the crowd's assumptions, and handily laying the foundation for the diverting result.

   Laying out the Comedic Reason:

   The arrangement starts with the foundation of the comedic premise, a urgent part that gives the setting to the humor to unfurl. This reason goes about as an aide, motioning toward the crowd the comedic scene they are going to navigate. It very well may be an engaging perception, an eccentric situation, or a smart curve on a natural subject, making way for what is to come.

   In stand-up satire, the initial lines of a routine frequently act as the arrangement, presenting the focal subject or reason that the humorist will investigate. This underlying second lays out an association with the crowd, welcoming them to go into the comedic world created by the entertainer. The reason turns into the anchor that grounds the forthcoming humor, making expectation and interest.

Astute Language and Pleasantry:

Inside the arrangement, the utilization of cunning language and pleasantry turns into an intense device for drawing in the crowd. Comics magnificently control words, making arrangements that play with language, risqué statement, or etymological subtleties. This phonetic artfulness adds a scholarly layer to the humor, welcoming the crowd to see the value in the mind implanted in the arrangement.

Consider the wit rich arrangements of comics like George Carlin or Steven Wright. Their arrangements frequently include etymological turns, astute expressing, or unforeseen associations between words. By utilizing language as a comedic instrument, these jokesters upgrade the arrangement, laying the basis for zingers that reverberate with both insight and humor.

Making Expectation:

A compelling arrangement is one that produces expectation inside the crowd, a feeling of hope that something hilarious is going to happen. This expectation is painstakingly developed through the selection of words, pacing, and the general tone of the arrangement. Humorists, essayists, and entertainers decisively construct expectation, realizing that the arrival of this strain will bring about chuckling.

In sitcoms, the arrangement frequently happens through situational parody where characters wind up in entertaining dilemmas. The arrangement makes expectation as watchers notice the unfurling occasions, anticipating that the humor should raise. The exemplary sitcom "I Love Lucy" succeeded in making arrangements through Lucy's misfortunes, keeping the crowd anxiously anticipating the unavoidable comedic goal.

Observational Humor and Appeal:

Numerous comedic arrangements draw their solidarity from observational humor, featuring the idiocies or peculiarities of regular daily existence. These arrangements reverberate with crowds by taking advantage of shared encounters and general bits of insight, making a feeling of appeal. The more appealing the arrangement, the more the crowd is leaned to draw in with the humor.

In stand-up satire, jokesters frequently make arrangements around appealing circumstances — unremarkable parts of day to day existence, social associations, or normal disappointments. Observational humor interfaces with crowds on an individual level, causing them to feel seen and comprehended. This mutual perspective intensifies the comedic influence when the zinger lands, changing appeal into aggregate chuckling.

Character Elements and Idiosyncrasies:

With regards to prearranged satire, arrangements are frequently complicatedly attached to the elements among characters and their special peculiarities. Each character turns into a possible wellspring of humor, and their connections set up for comedic minutes to unfurl. The arrangement includes presenting the characters, their mannerisms, and the potential for struggle or false impressions.

The sitcom "The Workplace" amazingly used character elements for comedic arrangements. The differentiating characters of characters like Michael Scott and Dwight Schrute made a ripe ground for humor. The arrangement frequently involved putting these characters in silly circumstances or investigating their eccentric ways to deal with office life, creating expectation for the comedic goals that followed.

Confusion and Shock:

A sign of a very much created arrangement is the component of confusion — an intentional redirection that drives the crowd down a specific way prior to astonishing them with a surprising turn. This unexpected component adds profundity to the arrangement, surprising the crowd and increasing the comedic effect of the resulting zinger.

Humorists frequently utilize confusion in stand-up schedules, guiding the crowd towards one assumption prior to undermining it with a cunning turn. The arrangement makes a psychological picture or expectation, and the humorist gains by this assumption by presenting a startling component. This component of shock turns into an incredible asset for keeping up with the crowd's commitment and guaranteeing that the humor stays new and eccentric.

Visual Components and Actual Satire:

In mediums like film and TV, the arrangement can reach out indeed to consolidate visual components and actual satire. Visual gags, droll humor, and overstated actual developments become necessary pieces of the arrangement, making expectation through the sheer ludicrousness or visual effect of the situation.

Consider the visual arrangements in quiet movies by legends like Charlie Chaplin. The actual parody and visual gags were unpredictably woven into the arrangements, depending on the expressiveness of non-verbal communication and the astute organization of visual components. These arrangements, absent any and all expressed words, imparted humor through the sly exchange of visuals and genuineness.

Social Editorial and Parody:

In certain cases, comedic arrangements dive into social editorial and parody, involving humor as a focal point to study cultural standards, patterns, or shows. These arrangements include introducing what is happening or situation that reflects parts of the social scene, welcoming the crowd to draw in with the humor on a more profound, provocative level.

Sarcastic comics frequently succeed in making arrangements that include social analysis. The arrangement turns into a vehicle for featuring the idiocies or logical inconsistencies inside society, involving humor for of inciting thought while inspiring giggling. This double capability of arrangements in parody adds to a layered and mentally invigorating comedic experience.

Timing and Beat:

The viability of a comedic arrangement is complicatedly attached to timing and mood. Joke artists and entertainers level up their skill to convey arrangements with flawless timing, figuring out that the pacing of words, stops, and in general cadence add to the development of expectation. The very much planned conveyance of arrangements guarantees that the crowd is prepared for the zinger.

In stand-up parody, timing is an expertise that comics constantly refine. The essential utilization of stops, the pacing of words, and an intense consciousness of the crowd's responses all add to the dominance of comedic timing. A very much coordinated arrangement makes a cadence that improves the comedic experience, making the possible zinger more significant.

2. **The Twist**

At the core of comedic narrating, the bend arises as a masterstroke, an essential move that turns the story on its head and drives the crowd into attacks of chuckling. Whether in stand-up schedules, sitcoms, movies, or writing, the turn is a story gadget that undermines assumptions, presents surprising components, and raises the comedic experience higher than ever.

Challenging Assumptions:

The substance of the turn lies in its capacity to surprise everyone. Comics and narrators handily set up a situation, directing the crowd along a specific story way. Nonetheless, when the crowd subsides into a feeling of consistency, the bend arises — an unanticipated new development or a startling disclosure that surprises everybody.

In stand-up satire, the curve is frequently the zinger, the second where the entertainer digresses from the expected goal and conveys an unforeseen wind that changes the arrangement into comedic gold. The progress of the bend depends on its capacity to amaze, producing chuckling by opposing the crowd's underlying assumptions.

Zingers and Disruption:

In the domain of parody, zingers are the thumping heart of the curve. The curve changes an apparently normal arrangement into a comedic disclosure, undermining the crowd's suspicions and conveying the zinger with greatest effect. The workmanship lies in the essential sending of the curve, guaranteeing that it resounds with the laid out comedic tone while offering a new and unforeseen point of view.

Think about the work of art "pull back and uncover" strategy frequently utilized in sitcoms. A person might portray what is happening, and the contort comes when the camera pulls back to uncover an unforeseen visual component, giving the zinger. This disruption of assumptions increases the humor, transforming what appeared to be direct into a comedic disclosure.

Visual Parody and Ridiculousness:

The curve tracks down a characteristic home in visual parody, where ridiculous and unforeseen components can be consistently coordinated. Visual gags, sight gags, and actual parody frequently depend on the wind to produce giggles. The juxtaposition of what is generally anticipated with what is introduced outwardly makes a superb discord that fills in as an impetus for giggling.

The movies of the Marx Siblings, known for their anarchic and silly humor, frequently consolidated visual turns. Groucho, Chico, and Harpo would participate in tricks where the normal results were undermined by the silliness of their activities.

The visual turns added layers to the humor as well as exhibited the brightness of integrating surprising components into the comedic story.

Incongruity and Inversions:

The turn as often as possible use incongruity and inversions, causing circumstances where the result is entirely against what the crowd expects. This play on assumptions adds intricacy to the comedic story, inciting chuckling through the sheer incongruity of the contort. The inversion of fortunes or the unforeseen outcomes of an arrangement add to the by and large comedic influence.

In writing, the curve can appear through amusing plot improvements or character inversions. A person's activities might prompt potentially negative side-effects, and the turn lies in the startling results that follow. This utilization of incongruity upgrades the comedic profundity, welcoming the crowd to see the value in the humor implanted in the unforeseen turns of the story.

Layering Humor and Callbacks:

The turn can possibly layer humor by expanding on laid out comedic components. Callbacks to prior arrangements or running gags can be consistently woven into the turn, making a feeling of progression and remunerating mindful crowd individuals. This layering of humor upgrades the lavishness of the comedic experience and adds an additional aspect to the bend.

Consider a sitcom where a repetitive person quality turns into a focal component in a wind. The callback to the laid out attribute gives progression as well as intensifies the humor as the curve unfurls. This exchange among callback and contort features the complexities of making comedic accounts that reverberate with crowds after some time.

Shock in Stand-up Parody:

In stand-up parody, the unexpected component of the curve is elevated by the immediate communication between the jokester and the crowd. Jokesters measure crowd responses, and the wind turns into a unique second where the unforeseen creates quick giggling. The component of shock, conveyed with faultless timing, changes the common into the unprecedented in the realm of stand-up.

The late Mitch Hedberg was an expert of shock in stand-up parody, frequently utilizing turns as ludicrous and startling zingers. His novel style included setting up commonplace situations and conveying zingers that took a dreamlike turn, leaving crowds in join. The unexpected consider Hedberg's turns displayed the force of startling humor in the stand-up type.

Mocking Turns and Social Editorial:

Past simple chuckling, the contort can be a vehicle for parody and social critique. Sarcastic turns include involving humor as a focal point to study cultural standards, shows, or patterns. By implanting the wind with parody, makers can inspire chuckling while at the same time inciting the crowd to ponder further layers of importance.

The enlivened series "The Simpsons" is prestigious for its ironical turns, where apparently harmless arrangements change into discourse on legislative issues, culture, and society. The curve turns into a device for both chuckling and reflection, displaying the flexibility of comedic narrating in resolving certifiable issues.

Acceleration and Unobtrusive Turns:

The curve can likewise appear through the heightening of humor inside a story. Unobtrusive turns through heightening craziness or the acquaintance of startling components contribute with the generally comedic force. The steady unfurling of comedic turns keeps the crowd connected with, anxiously expecting each new disclosure.

Consider crafted by comedic movie producer Edgar Wright, known for his utilization of visual and story acceleration. In films like "Shaun of the Dead" and "Hot Fluff," unpretentious turns through raising ludicrousness add to the comedic cadence. These turns shock the crowd as well as act as building blocks for bigger comedic settlements.

3. The Punchline

At the center of comedic creativity, the zinger is the crescendo, the snapshot of disclosure that changes expectation into loud chuckling. Across the assorted scene of satire — be it stand-up schedules, sitcoms, movies, or writing — the zinger is the gem in the comedic crown, conveying the startling with faultless timing, semantic artfulness, and a natural comprehension of the crowd's comedic sensibilities.

Timing as the Pith:

The zinger is, most importantly, a practice in timing. Whether spoken by a professional comic in front of an audience or conveyed through the exchange of characters in a sitcom, the outcome of a zinger depends on its very much adjusted appearance. The delay before the zinger, the beat that permits the crowd's expectation to construct, is just about as vital as the actual zinger. The jokesters' dominance lies in the capacity to explore this fleeting dance, making a comedic beat that finishes in the expertly coordinated zinger.

In the domain of stand-up parody, the connection among timing and zingers is a work of art regardless of anyone else's opinion. Humorists exploit the pregnant delay, permitting the crowd to hold tight the slope of assumption prior to diving into the surprising turn or disclosure. This coordination of time is the mysterious fixing that lifts a very much created arrangement into a noteworthy zinger.

Pleasantry and Phonetic Speculative chemistry:

The zinger is a semantic speculative chemistry, where words are employed with accuracy, making a mixture of humor that leaves the crowd in join. Pleasantry, jokes, and smart manners of speaking are the secrets to success, permitting comics to control language in manners that astonishment, entertain, and enchant.

Consider the exemplary illustration of a quip in a zinger. The cunning pun presents a double significance, surprising the crowd with its phonetic mastery. The zinger turns into a phonetic riddle, welcoming the crowd to delight in the mind and knowledge behind the comedic development.

Disruption and Shock:

A sign of a successful zinger is its capacity to undermine assumptions. The zinger takes the crowd on an excursion, driving them down a way of expectation set up by the former components of the comedic story. However, rather than showing up at the expected objective, the crowd is met with a superb shock — a turn that overcomes their presumption and produces giggling through the sheer suddenness of the disclosure.

In prearranged parody, the zinger frequently includes an inversion or disruption of an arrangement. A person's activities or the goal of a circumstance goes off in a strange direction, getting watchers unsuspecting. This component of shock is the impetus for the chuckling that follows, as the crowd gets a kick out of the shrewd deviation from the expected result.

Social Significance and Mutual perspective:

Zingers frequently draw on social references and common perspective, making a feeling of public giggling that resounds with different crowds. Comics tap into the aggregate encounters, standards, and subtleties of society, utilizing these social touchpoints to create zingers that rise above individual viewpoints and join crowds in giggling.

In sitcoms, social references become necessary to zingers. A very much coordinated reference to a recent development, a famous pattern, or a cultural idiosyncrasy adds a layer of appeal to the zinger. This mutual perspective intensifies the humor, making the zinger an extension that interfaces different crowd individuals through their normal social encounters.

Character-Based Humor:

The zinger frequently rises out of the profundities of character-based humor, where the eccentricities, defects, and peculiarities of people become rich wellsprings of comedic material. In sitcoms and stand-up schedules the same, noteworthy characters are characterized by their zingers — those snapshots of disclosure that epitomize the substance of their comedic personality.

Consider notorious characters like Sheldon Cooper from "The Theory of how things came to be." His zingers frequently emerge from his unconventionalities and inflexible adherence to schedule. The crowd expects these minutes, knowing that Sheldon's exceptional perspective will definitely prompt a zinger that catches the humor of his personality.

Zingers as Therapy:

Chuckling, prodded by a very much created zinger, fills in as a soothing delivery. The pressure worked through astute arrangements, phonetic play, and shock is diffused in the touchy delight of giggling. The zinger, in this sense, turns into a remedial device, offering a snapshot of rest from the afflictions of day to day existence and a common encounter that joins crowds in their aggregate entertainment.

In stand-up parody, jokesters frequently explore dim or testing subjects, utilizing zingers for the purpose of therapy. The unforeseen contort or sharp perception turns into a delivery valve, permitting the crowd to face troublesome subjects from the perspective of humor and track down comfort in shared chuckling.

Chapter 4

Finding Inspiration

Finding motivation, the flash that lights imagination, is a mysterious excursion extraordinary to every person. Whether you are a craftsman, essayist, performer, or anybody participated in an imaginative pursuit, the mission for motivation is a dynamic and frequently tricky cycle. It includes taking advantage of the wellspring of thoughts, drawing from different sources, and developing an outlook that encourages inventiveness. This investigation dives into the multi-layered nature of tracking down motivation, embracing the intrinsic difficulties and commending the groundbreaking force of imaginative knowledge.

The Powerful Idea of Motivation:

Motivation is a powerful power, ebbing and streaming like a waterway of inventiveness. It's anything but a steady, unsurprising stream but instead a liquid energy that can flood out of the blue or retreat all of a sudden. Understanding and tolerating the powerful idea of motivation is pivotal in exploring the innovative strategy. Now and then, motivation strikes like a lightning bolt, and thoughts pour forward easily. Different times, it requires patient development and conscious investigation.

The painter gazing at a fresh start, the essayist confronting a vacant page, or the performer with a quiet instrument — all offer a typical mission for motivation. It's a continuous discourse with the dream, a complicated dance between the maker and the imaginative power that drives the creative excursion forward.

Perception and Care:

One of the essential wellsprings of motivation lies in the craft of perception. Drawing in with the world with a sharp feeling of care opens up a huge repository of boosts that can set off imaginative contemplations. Noticing the complexities of regular day to day existence, the play of light and shadow, the subtleties of human association, or the examples in nature — all give grub to imaginative investigation.

Specialists like Vincent van Gogh tracked down motivation in the energetic shades of nature, catching the substance of scenes with distinctive brushstrokes. Scholars frequently draw motivation from noticing individuals, connections, or cultural elements. The demonstration of carefully captivating with the world turns into a well of motivation, permitting makers to track down excellence and interest in the apparently commonplace.

Interest and Investigation:

Interest is the motor that drives the investigation of groundbreaking thoughts and points of view. Embracing a mentality of interest includes an eagerness to wander into the obscure, to seek clarification on pressing issues, and to challenge predispositions. It is the longing to disentangle the secrets of the world and to search out the unseen.

Researchers, craftsmen, and creators the same are powered by a feeling of interest. The space expert investigating the universe, the stone carver exploring different avenues regarding new materials, or the researcher diving into strange domains of information — all are driven by a voracious interest that moves them to push limits and uncover the uncommon.

Perusing and Mixture:

Writing, a mother lode of human experience and creative mind, has been a perpetual wellspring of motivation. Perusing across different types opens makers to a huge number of points of view, styles, and thoughts. It expands the imaginative range, mixing the brain with a rich embroidery of stories and ideas.

Journalists frequently credit their ravenous perusing propensities as a huge consider tracking down motivation. The capacity to navigate different scholarly scenes — from exemplary writing to contemporary works, from fiction to verifiable — adds to a more diverse and nuanced innovative reasonableness. This variety of impacts improves the potential for interesting and imaginative manifestations.

Embracing Difficulties and Distress:

Motivation frequently rises out of the cauldron of difficulties and inconvenience. It is during snapshots of difficulty that the human soul is tried and, perplexingly, powered. Innovative forward leaps habitually emerge when confronted with impediments or pushed past one's usual range of familiarity.

The stone worker etching away at a difficult block of stone, the performer wrestling with a perplexing melodic sythesis, or the business visionary exploring the vulnerabilities of another endeavor — all stand up to difficulties that, thus, become wellsprings of motivation. Embracing distress turns into an impetus for development and inventiveness.

Reflection and Isolation:

In the midst of the commotion of the cutting edge world, snapshots of isolation and reflection become fundamental for sustaining motivation. The innovative brain frequently requires a peaceful space for reflection, permitting contemplations to permeate, thoughts to gestate, and bits of knowledge to solidify. It is at these times of tranquility that the murmurs of motivation are generally perceptible.

Journalists frequently retreat to calm spaces, craftsmen track down comfort in their studios, and masterminds search out isolated conditions for thought. In the hug of isolation, the brain can meander unreservedly, associating dissimilar considerations and framing the mosaic of motivation.

Cooperation and Trade of Thoughts:

Motivation flourishes in the rich ground of coordinated effort and the trading of thoughts. Connecting with other imaginative personalities, taking part in discussions, and partaking in cooperative tasks can be a wellspring of new viewpoints and creative ideas.

The cooperative energy of a jazz gathering, the brotherhood of a meeting to generate new ideas, or the coordinated effort between interdisciplinary craftsmen — all epitomize the force of aggregate imagination. The cross-fertilization of thoughts that happens in cooperative undertakings frequently ignites new and unforeseen pathways of motivation.

Gaining from Different Disciplines:

Drawing motivation from disciplines outside one's own is a sign of innovative diversity. The standards of configuration illuminating engineering, the cadenced examples of dance affecting music sythesis, or the numerical accuracy motivating visual craftsmanship — all represent the cross-preparation of thoughts across assorted areas.

Development every now and again emerges at the crossing point of various fields. Researchers might track down motivation in standards of plan, and specialists might draw from the designs of arithmetic. This interdisciplinary methodology improves the imaginative scene, cultivating the development of novel and limit opposing manifestations.

Social Submersion and Variety:

Drenching oneself in various societies and embracing variety gives a rich wellspring of motivation. Openness to changed customs, customs, and points of view upgrades the profundity and expansiveness of innovative articulation. It challenges assumptions and empowers a more comprehensive and extensive way to deal with inventiveness.

Travel, social trades, and commitment with assorted networks expand the material whereupon motivation is painted. The producer investigating stories from various societies, the gourmet expert exploring different avenues regarding worldwide foods, or the essayist drawing characters from assorted foundations — all epitomize the significant effect of social submersion on imaginative undertakings.

Nature as a Wellspring of Motivation:

The regular world, with its spectacular excellence and multifaceted environments, has for some time been a dream for innovative personalities. Craftsmen, artists, and performers frequently go to nature for motivation, catching its pith in their works. The quiet scenes, the cadenced examples of seasons, and the biodiversity of verdure — all summon a feeling of miracle that sparkles inventive investigation.

Tree huggers like John Muir tracked down motivation in the flawless wild, communicating their veneration for nature through words and activities. Also, craftsmen like Georgia O'Keeffe drew motivation from the dynamic shades and states of blossoms. Nature's significant impact on innovativeness is a demonstration of the harmonious connection between the regular world and the human creative mind.

4.1 Drawing from Personal Experiences

Drawing from individual encounters is a significant and personal excursion that energizes the innovative flow across different creative domains. Whether in writing, visual expressions, music, or some other type of articulation, the realness got from individual experiences, feelings, and reflections pervades imaginative works with a one of a kind profundity and reverberation. This investigation digs into the perplexing interchange between private encounters and creative articulation, unwinding the groundbreaking force of transforming life into workmanship.

The Material of Personal Articulation:

Craftsmen frequently utilize their lives as a material, making works of art that spring from the well of individual encounters. Self-portraying articulation permits makers to wind around stories, paint pictures, or create tunes that are profoundly private as well as generally engaging. By sharing their own accounts, specialists interface with crowds on a significant level, encouraging compassion and understanding.

In writing, scholars like Sylvia Plath and Maya Angelou transformed the woven artwork of their lives into wonderful reflections. Plath's "The Ringer Container" draws intensely from her own battles with emotional well-being, offering a crude and instinctive depiction that resounds with perusers confronting comparable difficulties. Angelou's self-portraying works, including "I Know Why the Confined Bird Sings," dig into her encounters with prejudice, injury, and win, making a scholarly inheritance that rises above individual stories.

The Close to home Reverberation of Individual Accounts:

Individual encounters are a wellspring of feelings, and taking advantage of these profound supplies enhances creative articulation. Whether it's the delight of affection, the distress of misfortune, the adventure of accomplishment, or the torment of disappointment, specialists channel these feelings into their work, making pieces that bring out instinctive reactions from crowds.

Music, as an all inclusive language of feeling, frequently draws vigorously from individual encounters. From Adele's tragic songs brought into the world from the cinders of bombed connections to Bruce Springsteen's hymns mirroring the battles of the common laborers, the close to home reverberation of individual stories in music is irrefutable. The legitimacy of these encounters permits audience members to interface with the music on a significant close to home level, manufacturing a bond that rises above the limits of time and culture.

Therapy Through Imaginative Articulation:

For some specialists, the demonstration of making an interpretation of individual encounters into craftsmanship fills in as a soothing delivery. Composing, painting, creating, or some other inventive pursuit turns into a remedial source for handling feelings, figuring out the intricacies of life, and exploring the wild oceans of human experience.

In visual expressions, painters like Frida Kahlo changed their agony and enduring into strong masterpieces. Kahlo's self-representations, frequently portraying her physical and profound battles, are materials as well as windows into her inward world. The most common way of making these craftsmanships turned into a type of close to home therapy, permitting Kahlo to defy and change her aggravation through the demonstration of painting.

Exploring the Profundities of Human Intricacy:

Human encounters are innately intricate, set apart by a bunch of feelings, connections, and difficulties. Specialists, as sharp eyewitnesses and translators of the human condition, dive into these intricacies, offering nuanced depictions that catch the pith of being human.

In the domain of writing, the Russian writer Fyodor Dostoevsky dove into the profundities of human brain science and existential anxiety in works like "Wrongdoing and Discipline" and "The Siblings Karamazov." Drawing from his own battles, Dostoevsky investigated topics of ethical quality, responsibility, and recovery, creating characters that wrestle with the intricacies of their own reality. His stories, established in private encounters, keep on resounding across time and social partitions.

Building Genuine Associations with Crowds:

Legitimacy is an attractive power in creative articulation. Crowds are attracted to works that vibe certifiable and valid, and the genuineness got from individual encounters lays out a strong association between the maker and the eyewitness. At the point when craftsmen share their weaknesses, wins, and hardships, they welcome crowds into a common space of understanding and compassion.

Professional comics, seasoned veterans at transforming individual accounts into comedic gold, frequently construct their schedules around regular encounters. Entertainers like Richard Pryor and Eddie Murphy, by imparting their own experiences to race, relational intricacies, and cultural standards, make humor that isn't just silly yet in addition profoundly smart. The realness of their accounts permits crowds to giggle at the jokes as well as at the common idiocies of the human experience.

The Convergence of Fiction and Reality:

Indeed, even in works of fiction, the implantation of individual encounters adds a layer of validness that reverberates with perusers and watchers. Essayists frequently draw motivation from genuine occasions, individuals, and feelings, integrating them into fictitious accounts to make universes that vibe clear and veritable.

In the dream classification, creators like J.K. Rowling wove components of her own battles and wins into the Harry Potter series. The subjects of kinship, flexibility, and the fight among great and fiendish in the mysterious domain mirror Rowling's own excursion. By imbuing her own encounters into a fantastical story, she made a generally darling story that rises above the limits old enough and culture.

Difficulties and Weaknesses as Impetuses for Craftsmanship:

Difficulties, mishaps, and weaknesses are innate parts of the human experience as well as strong impetuses for creative articulation.

At the point when craftsmen face difficulty, whether it be private, cultural, or existential, the extraordinary speculative chemistry of transforming difficulties into craftsmanship starts.

The dramatist Tennessee Williams, through works like "A Trolley Named Want" and "The Glass Zoological garden," wrestled with his own subtle conflicts and the cultural tensions of his time. Williams involved his weaknesses as a dramatist, investigating subjects of emotional well-being, relational intricacies, and the delicacy of the human mind. In doing as such, he made immortal works that reverberate with crowds defying comparable difficulties.

Embracing Multidimensionality:

The multidimensionality of human experience permits craftsmen to draw from a huge supply of recollections, feelings, and points of view. This lavishness adds to the diverse idea of imaginative articulation, empowering makers to investigate different features of their own day to day routines and the existences of others.

In photography, craftsmen like Diane Arbus caught the complex parts of human life. Arbus' representations, frequently portraying people on the edges of society, uncover a significant compassion and interest in the variety of human encounters. By investigating the intricacies of character, contrast, and association, Arbus' photos rise above simple documentation, becoming windows into the horde stories that unfurl in the embroidered artwork of life.

1. **Turning Mishaps into Humor**

   Transforming setbacks into humor is an exceptional speculative chemistry that changes life's unforeseen staggers and bungles into comedic gold. Whether in the domain of stand-up parody, narrating, or regular discussions, the capacity to find humor in misfortunes eases up the mind-set as well as makes a common encounter that reverberates with crowds. This investigation digs into the craft of transforming setbacks into humor, unwinding the elements of comedic narrating that rise up out of the wonderful tumult of life's bungles.

   The All inclusiveness of Incidents:

   Incidents are a widespread part of the human experience. From humiliating minutes and off-kilter experiences to startling bits of destiny, everybody has an assortment of stories that include exploring the unusual landscape of life. The comprehensiveness of setbacks turns into a rich ground for humor, as crowds can connect with the intrinsic unusualness and incidental idiocy of the human excursion.

   Professional comics, specifically, influence the comprehensiveness of accidents to produce associations with their crowds. By sharing individual stories of misfortunes, jokesters welcome giggling on their own as well as at the common idiocies of the human condition.

   This public giggling makes a connection between the entertainer and the crowd, as everybody perceives the engaging idea of life's hiccups.

   The Weakness of Validness:

   Transforming setbacks into humor requires a readiness to embrace weakness and legitimacy. At the point when narrators, jokesters, or people relate their own slips up, imperfections, and quirks, they open a window into their genuine selves. This weakness, nowhere near lessening one's standing, charms them to the crowd, encouraging a feeling of association in view of shared humankind.

Jokester Hannah Gadsby, in her historic exceptional "Nanette," handily transforms individual mishaps into piercing and funny accounts. Through genuine narrating, Gadsby evokes chuckling as well as difficulties the customary assumptions for parody. Her eagerness to uncover weakness makes a strong reverberation, welcoming the crowd to ponder their own encounters while delighting in the humor brought into the world from credibility.

Timing and Conveyance in Satire:

In the domain of satire, timing and conveyance are critical components while transforming disasters into humor. The very much created zinger, conveyed with flawless timing, can change an off-kilter circumstance into a comedic win. Joke artists frequently utilize the component of shock, the surprising turn, or the beautifully planned respite to enhance the humor inborn in setbacks.

Consider a stand-up routine where a humorist describes an incident including a closet breakdown. The planning of the zinger, maybe a sharp remark about the craziness of the circumstance, transforms expected humiliation into loud giggling. The fragile dance of timing and conveyance permits jokesters to explore the scarcely discernible difference among inconvenience and entertainment, changing incidents into noteworthy comedic minutes.

Misrepresentation and Poetic exaggeration:

Distortion and poetic exaggeration are amazing assets in the stockpile of comedic narrating. By intensifying the subtleties of an incident, makers can raise the humor and idiocy of the circumstance. This comedic adornment permits crowds to move away from the truth of the incident and draw in with the misrepresented story for greatest comedic impact.

In narrating, creators like Imprint Twain excelled at misrepresentation to transform disasters into ageless stories. Twain's records of his misfortunes, whether exploring the Mississippi Stream or prospecting for gold, are injected with a silly distortion that rises above the particular conditions. The amazing idea of these accounts adds layers of humor, welcoming perusers to delight in the comedic self importance of the setbacks.

The Force of Viewpoint:

Transforming setbacks into humor frequently relies on a change in context. What may be seen as a disaster at the time can, with the right outlining, become a wellspring of entertainment. Entertainers, narrators, and people proficient at this craftsmanship perceive that how a story is informed shapes its diverting potential. The decision of viewpoint, whether humble or observational, adds to the comedic focal point through which the incident is seen.

In regular discussions, the force of point of view is obvious when somebody describes a disaster with a mindful and entertaining turn. The capacity to step back, see the master plan, and find the comedic point permits people to explore humiliation as well as to change it into a wellspring of shared giggling effectively.

Social Analysis through Accidents:

Transforming setbacks into humor can rise above simple giggling and act as a vehicle for social critique. Comedic narrating frequently includes featuring cultural standards, assumptions, or idiocies from the perspective of individual misfortunes. By involving disasters as a material for editorial, makers connect with crowds in reflections on more extensive topics while evoking chuckling.

The ironical brightness of setback based humor is exemplified in sitcoms like "Control Your Excitement," where Larry David's personality explores a progression of social disasters and tactless act. Every misfortune turns into a diverting discourse on friendly shows, behavior, and the complexities of human connection.

From the perspective of satire, incidents become a mirror reflecting cultural peculiarities.

Flexibility and Strengthening:

As well as inspiring chuckling, transforming setbacks into humor can be an enabling demonstration of flexibility. By recovering responsibility for's stumbles and finding humor in misfortune, people state organization over their stories. This versatility permits them not exclusively to defeat humiliation yet additionally to change incidents into accounts of win and self-awareness.

The entertainer Ali Wong, in her stand-up specials, frequently transforms individual disasters and weaknesses into engaging accounts. Her plain and amusing conversations about pregnancy, parenthood, and connections resound as comedic accounts as well as articulations of strength and strengthening. Through chuckling, Wong explores the difficulties of existence with beauty and legitimacy.

2. **Observational Comedy**

Observational satire, a sort that blossoms with distinctly noticing and entertainingly taking apart the particulars of daily existence, remains as a demonstration of the comedic splendor saw as in the conventional. Established in the craft of intense discernment and engaging bits of knowledge, observational satire changes the unremarkable into comedic gold. This investigation digs into the subtleties of observational parody, looking at its establishments, the craft of sharp perception, and the remarkable capacity to inspire giggling from the texture of our everyday encounters.

Groundworks of Observational Satire:

At the core of observational satire lies the acknowledgment that humor is much of the time tracked down in the subtleties of our common reality. Entertainers who spend significant time in this sort influence their capacity to acutely notice their general surroundings, separating humor from the ordinary events that could some way or another slip through the cracks. The underpinnings of observational satire lay on the widespread idea of these perceptions — ordinary circumstances, social eccentricities, and human way of behaving that reverberate across different crowds.

Jerry Seinfeld, frequently hailed as an expert of observational satire, constructed his profession by transforming the details of life into comedic splendor. From the idiocies of breakfast cereals to the subtleties of social decorum, Seinfeld's humor is grounded in the ordinary encounters that associate all of us. The appeal of his observational parody lies in the common acknowledgment of the natural, causing the crowd to feel like dynamic members in the humor.

The Craft of Sharp Perception:

Observational jokesters have a remarkable range of abilities that spins around the craft of sharp perception. They examine the world with an insightful eye, separating humor from the ordinary and introducing it such that prompts crowds to gesture in acknowledgment. The capacity to see unobtrusive subtleties, question cultural standards, and feature the idiocies of day to day existence characterizes the observational joke artist's art.

Consider crafted by Ellen DeGeneres, whose observational satire frequently fixates on the peculiarities of human way of behaving. From the idiosyncrasies of current innovation to the quirks of looking for garments, DeGeneres raises the normal to the remarkable through her sharp observational focal point. Her humor isn't simply about the subjects she picks however about the clever and appealing manner by which she analyzes them.

The Force of Appeal:

Observational satire infers quite a bit of its power from appeal. At the point when crowds perceive their own encounters in an entertainer's perceptions, an association is fashioned. The common affirmation of the natural makes a quick compatibility, cultivating a climate where giggling turns into a collective encounter. Observational comics act as courses, articulating shared opinions and giving a funny focal point through which crowds view their own lives.

Jokester and entertainer Kevin Hart frequently injects his stand-up schedules with observational humor that mirrors the shared characteristics of the human experience. Whether tending to the difficulties of nurturing, the elements of connections, or the idiocies of social cooperations, Hart's interesting bits of knowledge resound with crowds of different foundations. In the comprehensiveness of his perceptions, chuckling turns into a binding together power that rises above individual contrasts.

Transforming Unremarkable into Phenomenal:

Observational jokesters have the ability to interest to transform the ordinary into the unprecedented. Regular events that may be excused as normal or mediocre are changed into comedic pearls through the jokester's point of view. This change includes considering the humor in the common to be well as introducing it in a manner that hoists its comedic esteem.

Louis C.K., known for his open and frequently humble observational parody, succeeds at transforming the ordinary into boisterous giggling. His appearance on the difficulties of nurturing, the idiocies of innovation, and the subtleties of social elements resound exactly in light of the fact that they get humor from the texture of regular daily existence. By offering a new point of view on the apparently cliché, C.K. shows the way that the normal can turn into an unprecedented wellspring of comedic motivation.

Social Analysis through Perception:

Observational satire frequently fills in as a vehicle for social editorial. By examining cultural standards, social patterns, and human way of behaving, joke artists can feature fundamental insights and incite thought while evoking giggling. The shrewd perceptions of comics become a mirror mirroring the aggregate eccentricities of society.

George Carlin, an unbelievable observational comic, used his sharp perceptions to convey intense social discourse. His schedules took apart language, governmental issues, and the idiocies of current life, offering a viewpoint that went past simple diversion. Carlin's capacity to involve humor as a focal point for evaluating society represents how observational parody can rise above chuckling, turning into a stage for wise reflections on the world we possess.

Social Subtleties and Variety in Perception:

Observational satire, when rehearsed with social responsiveness, has the ability to investigate the subtleties of different encounters. Humorists who explore social perceptions do as such with a consciousness of the different points of view inside their crowd. By featuring social characteristics, customs, and shared encounters, these comics commend the rich embroidery of humankind.

Russell Peters, in his kind of observational parody, digs into social variety with mind and humor. By investigating the complexities of various nationalities and social connections, Peters welcomes chuckling that emerges not from generalizations but rather from the acknowledgment of shared encounters inside different networks. In doing as such, he exhibits the capability of observational parody to connect social holes and encourage grasping through humor.

4.2 Exploring Cultural Humor

Social humor, a dynamic and multi-layered kind, fills in as an impression of the rich embroidery of human variety. Established in the quirks, customs, and shared encounters of various societies, this type of satire has the capacity to both engage and illuminate. This investigation digs into the subtleties of social humor, analyzing its part in encouraging comprehension, exploring cultural intricacies, and commending the assorted articulations of giggling across the globe.

The Mosaic of Social Humor:

Social humor is a mosaic that draws motivation from the particular qualities and subtleties of different social orders. Jokesters, authors, and entertainers capable in this classification influence social components, like language, customs, and social elements, to create stories that resound with crowds acquainted with those particular social references.

This rich embroidery of humor mirrors the kaleidoscope of human encounters and points of view.

Consider crafted by Mindy Kaling, whose comedic narrating frequently consolidates components of her Indian legacy. Kaling consistently winds around social references, familial accounts, and perceptions about social assumptions into her stories. Through her humor, she evokes giggling as well as furnishes crowds with a window into the intricacies and enjoyments of exploring social convergences.

Cultivating Grasping through Giggling:

One of the significant parts of social humor lies in its capacity to encourage grasping between various networks. By investigating and giggling at the social quirks and shared characteristics that characterize us, people from different foundations can settle on something worth agreeing on. Shared giggling turns into a scaffold, interfacing individuals across etymological, geographic, and social partitions.

The satire of Hasan Minhaj, known for his show "Loyalist Act," represents the capability of social humor to advance comprehension. Minhaj dives into subjects going from migration to global legislative issues, implanting his satire with individual stories and social references. Through humor, he engages as well as teaches, offering bits of knowledge into the encounters of minimized networks and encouraging sympathy among crowds.

Exploring Social Intricacies:

Social humor frequently fills in as a navigational device through the intricacies of cultural standards, generalizations, and personality. Entertainers adroit in this kind use humor to dismantle assumptions, challenge generalizations, and proposition nuanced points of view on social elements. The comedic focal point turns into a vehicle for destroying hindrances and welcoming crowds to rethink their suspicions.

Dave Chappelle, an expert of social parody, handily explores the intricacies of race, class, and cultural assumptions in his satire. Through portrays like "The Racial Draft" and "Dark Hedge," Chappelle faces racial generalizations and cultural disparities with humor that is both provocative and boisterous. His capacity to address delicate themes through satire shows the way that social humor can be a powerful device for social editorial and exchange.

Observing Social Variety:

At its center, social humor is a festival of variety. It gives a stage to networks to delight in their exceptional practices, dialects, and customs, while welcoming others to partake in the delight of social lavishness. This festival goes past generalizations, offering real looks into the liveliness of various societies.

Russell Peters, in his worldwide parody visits, celebrates social variety with an irresistible humor that rises above borders. Peters draws from his own encounters as a Canadian of Indian plunge, drawing in crowds with jokes that reverberate across different social foundations. His capacity to settle on something worth agreeing on in the variety of human encounters highlights the bringing together force of social humor.

Exploring Restrictions with Humor:

Social humor frequently explores the fragile territory of cultural restrictions, giving a space to conversations that may be trying in different settings. Jokesters skilled in this type use humor as a device to address delicate subjects, challenge standards, and brief crowds to address imbued convictions. The comedic stage turns into a gathering for pushing limits while welcoming chuckling that rises above cultural limitations.

Crafted by Margaret Cho, known for her limit pushing satire, embodies how social humor can explore restrictions. Cho bravely resolves issues of race, orientation, and sexuality in her satire, utilizing humor to destroy generalizations and challenge cultural assumptions. Her capacity to inject untouchable subjects with humor makes a space for exchange and reflection.

Social Humor in a Globalized World:

In an undeniably interconnected world, social humor takes on new aspects as it crosses borders and resounds with crowds across different social settings. Jokesters who explore this worldwide scene frequently track down humor in the common encounters of globalization, social combination, and the impact of customs.

The parody of Michael McIntyre, an English comic known for his observational humor, mirrors the globalized idea of social satire. While established in English culture, McIntyre's parody reverberates with crowds overall as he cleverly investigates the normal encounters of current life, from nurturing difficulties to mechanical idiocies. His capacity to find comprehensiveness in social explicitness shows the way that social humor can rise above geographic limits.

1. **Satirizing Social Norms**

   Parody, a type of humor that utilizes incongruity, scorn, and misrepresentation, fills in as a strong focal point through which normal practices can be examined and studied. By featuring the idiocies and logical inconsistencies inborn in cultural assumptions, mocking parody turns into a vehicle for social critique and a method for rocking the boat. This investigation dives into the specialty of parodying normal practices, inspecting how entertainers and authors use humor to enlighten cultural idiocies, brief reflection, and flash discussions about the shows that shape our lives.

   The Pith of Parody:

   At its center, parody is a method of articulation that looks to uncover and scrutinize human imprudence and cultural deficiencies. Sarcastic humor works through a blend of mind, incongruity, and embellishment, giving makers an instrument to analyze and remark on the standards, values, and ways of behaving that characterize a given society. This type of parody isn't just engaging yet additionally fills in as a mirror mirroring the peculiarities and inconsistencies of the world we occupy.

   Crafted by Jonathan Quick, especially "An Unobtrusive Proposition," embody the quintessence of mocking composition. Quick, in this paper, utilizes an apparently serious proposition — pushing for the utilization of newborn children as an answer for neediness — to ridicule the hardness of English strategies toward the Irish. The stunning proposition is a vehicle for Quick's gnawing scrutinize of the dehumanizing impacts of frontier rule and monetary double-dealing.

Testing Shows through Misrepresentation:

Misrepresentation is a sign of parody, permitting makers to intensify components of reality to a mark of silliness. By amplifying the elements of cultural standards, parody welcomes crowds to scrutinize the rationale and reasoning behind acknowledged shows. Through this exaggerative focal point, comics and journalists can uncover the inborn inconsistencies and ambiguities that frequently get away from notice in the everyday practice of day to day existence.

In the domain of stand-up parody, George Carlin was a pro at utilizing embellishment to mock normal practices. His everyday practice on the "Pursuit of happiness" analyzed the cultural assumptions encompassing achievement, homeownership, and commercialization. Through humor, Carlin uplifted the ludicrousness of unchallenged standards, empowering crowds to reexamine their points of view on the quest for satisfaction and the American lifestyle.

Incongruity as a Rebellious Instrument:

Parody frequently depends on incongruity as a rebellious instrument to convey implications that vary from the clear. The hole between what is said and what is implied permits humorists to make layers of importance, constraining crowds to take part in decisive reasoning. This utilization of incongruity engages as well as moves people to scrutinize the authenticity of winning standards. The TV series "The Simpsons," made by Matt Groening, has been a longstanding illustration of mocking satire utilizing incongruity. The imaginary town of Springfield fills in as a microcosm of American culture, and the show mocks a great many social issues through the existences of its characters. The incongruity lies in the hole between the apparently standard existences of the characters and the significant cultural scrutinizes implanted in the story.

Exposing Lip service and Twofold Principles:

One of parody's powerful capabilities is exposing pietism and twofold guidelines inside cultural standards. By comparing the beliefs upheld by a general public with the activities of its people or foundations, parody uncovered the disharmony between maintained values and real way of behaving. This openness can be an impetus for reflection and a call for change.

Crafted by Imprint Twain, especially "The Experiences of Huckleberry Finn," exhibit how parody can expose cultural deceptions. Twain's portrayal of the person Ruler, a misrepresentation who professes to be a duke, fills in as a blistering scrutinize of the assumptions and moral chapter 11 of the prior to the war Southern culture. Twain's parody uncovered the inconsistencies between the declared Christian qualities and the real direct of people in a general public saturated with prejudice and disparity.

Social Analysis through Farce:

Spoof, a type of parody that mirrors the style of a specific classification or work, is one more method through which normal practices can be parodied. By emulating and overstating the shows of a given structure, makers can offer a clever editorial on cultural assumptions, standards, and social peculiarities.

The movie "Bursting Seats," coordinated by Mel Streams, remains as an exemplary illustration of satire utilized for social editorial. Streams, from the perspective of a Western parody, ridicules prejudice, generalizations, and social conflicts. The film's comedic distortion and disruption of customary Western sayings act as a vehicle for addressing winning perspectives and standards, pushing crowds to face awkward bits of insight.

Catalyzing Change through Giggling:

While parody frequently features the imperfections and idiocies of normal practices, it can likewise act as an impetus for change. By inciting chuckling and reflection, parody welcomes people to reevaluate their points of view, rock the boat, and imagine an all the more and impartial society. The groundbreaking force of parody lies in its capacity to draw in hearts and brains through the widespread language of humor.

In the contemporary scene, entertainers like John Oliver use parody as a device for cultural study. Through his show "Last Week This evening," Oliver utilizes humor, mind, and top to bottom investigation to handle squeezing social and policy centered issues. The show's portions, frequently joining parody with analytical reporting, point not exclusively to engage yet additionally to rouse mindfulness and activity among watchers.

2. **Cross-Cultural Comedy**

Multifaceted parody, a great convergence of humor and social variety, rises above borders, uniting individuals through giggling that reverberates across various foundations and encounters. In the domain of parody, where shared chuckling structures a general language, multifaceted satire turns into a strong vehicle for encouraging grasping, destroying generalizations, and commending the extravagance of human variety.

The Worldwide Embroidered artwork of Parody:

Parody has the exceptional capacity to cross social limits, settling on something worth agreeing on in the common encounters, eccentricities, and idiocies that characterize the human condition. Multifaceted parody, specifically, winds around together strings from various social textures, making a dynamic and comprehensive embroidery of humor. Entertainers skilled in this classification explore the complexities of assorted societies, making stories that extension holes and welcome crowds to see the value in the humor in the mosaic of human encounters.

Russell Peters, known for his worldwide satire visits, embodies the quintessence of diverse parody. Peters, who is of Indian plunge and experienced childhood in Canada, capably integrates components from different social foundations into his schedules. By drawing on assorted encounters, Peters makes humor that rises above borders, reverberating with crowds around the world. His capacity to find the widespread in the particular epitomizes how diverse parody can make associations that go past geological and social partitions.

Destroying Generalizations with Humor:

One of the strong elements of diverse satire is its capacity to destroy generalizations through humor. By defying social generalizations head-on and involving them as comedic material, entertainers challenge assumptions and cultivate a more profound comprehension of various societies. The chuckling evoked by such parody turns into a device for separating obstructions and dispersing misguided judgments.

The satire of Hasan Minhaj, especially in his show "Loyalist Act," draws in with multifaceted humor to challenge generalizations and proposition nuanced viewpoints. Minhaj, who is of Indian-Muslim legacy, utilizes his foundation to address misinterpretations about his way of life and religion. Through humor, he incapacitates generalizations as well as welcomes crowds to see the common humankind past social contrasts.

Exploring Social Subtleties:

Multifaceted parody explores the complicated subtleties of different societies, investigating the nuances and peculiarities that make each culture exceptional. Jokesters who succeed in this class show a sharp comprehension of social elements, permitting them to energetically feature the peculiarities and complexities that may be lost in interpretation. The capacity to explore these subtleties adds to the legitimacy and appeal of culturally diverse satire.

The comedic pair Key and Peele, made out of Keegan-Michael Key and Jordan Peele, unbelievably explores social subtleties in their portrayals. Through their humor, Key and Peele dive into issues of race, personality, and social associations, giving sagacious critique while inspiring giggling. Their portrayals feature the lavishness of multifaceted parody, where a nuanced comprehension of social elements improves the comedic experience.

Observing Social Wealth:

At its center, multifaceted parody is a festival of the lavishness and variety of human societies. Comics who embrace this sort praise the practices, dialects, and customs that shape the mosaic of humankind. The humor turns into a scaffold that interfaces individuals, welcoming them to delight in the distinctions that make each culture exceptional.

Crafted by Ali Wong, whose satire frequently investigates her Asian-American personality, is a festival of social lavishness. Wong's humor, established in her encounters as a lady of Asian plunge, offers a special viewpoint that reverberates with crowds across social foundations.

Through her comedic focal point, Wong praises the intricacies of personality, testing the thought of a solitary, solid social experience.

Building Scaffolds through Chuckling:

Culturally diverse satire fills in as an amazing asset for building spans between various networks. Giggling, as a common encounter, makes a feeling of association and understanding that rises above social partitions. In reality as we know it where social variety is a strength, diverse satire turns into an extension that welcomes individuals to associate, appreciate, and track down euphoria in the mosaic of worldwide societies.

The stand-up parody of Eddie Izzard epitomizes the scaffold building capability of diverse satire. Izzard, known for his dreamlike and observational humor, consistently integrates social references from different nations into his schedules. By drawing in with different societies, Izzard encourages a feeling of worldwide brotherhood through giggling, welcoming crowds to see the value in the humor that rises above public lines.

Chapter 5

The Language of Laughter

The language of chuckling, a general and perplexing type of correspondence, rises above social, semantic, and social limits, winding around an embroidery of human association. From the loud roars reverberating through satire clubs to the unobtrusive laughs partook in regular discussions, chuckling fills in as a powerful language that conveys euphoria, understanding, and a common appreciation for the lighter parts of life. This investigation digs into the multi-layered elements of the language of chuckling, analyzing its social varieties, mental underpinnings, and its part in encouraging social bonds across the different scenes of human experience.

Social Varieties in Chuckling:

Chuckling, as a language, is rich with social subtleties that mirror the variety of human articulations. Various societies have one of a kind styles of humor and particular triggers for chuckling, impacted by verifiable, cultural, and etymological settings. Understanding these social varieties in chuckling is much the same as translating a language verbally expressed with subtleties, emphases, and social codes.

In Japan, for example, chuckling is frequently joined by nuance and limitation, mirroring the social worth put on congruity and staying away from disturbance. Contrastingly, the rowdy giggling pervasive in American stand-up parody clubs mirrors a culture that supports individual articulation and a more clear arrival of feelings. The language of chuckling, in its social variety, turns into a mirror mirroring the qualities and standards that impact social orders.

Mental Underpinnings of Chuckling:

Digging into the brain research of chuckling uncovers the perplexing interchange of feelings, social elements, and mental cycles that underlie this general articulation. Giggling isn't simply a reflex; a complex social and close to home sign conveys a scope of messages, from entertainment to kinship and even distress.

Clinician Robert Provine's exploration on giggling features its social nature, stressing that most chuckling is a social way of behaving that happens during communications with others. Shared chuckling fortifies social bonds, flagging a feeling of common perspective and common delight. The infectious idea of chuckling, where one individual's giggling can set off giggling in others, addresses the social synchrony worked with by this common language.

Chuckling likewise goes about as a therapeutic delivery, permitting people to explore pressure, strain, and distress. The physiological impacts of chuckling, including the arrival of endorphins and the decrease of pressure chemicals, add to its helpful characteristics. The language of giggling, in this mental setting, turns into a device for profound guideline and public prosperity.

Giggling as Friendly Paste:

Giggling's job as friendly paste is clear in its capacity to encourage associations and fortify relational connections. Shared chuckling makes a feeling of fellowship and having a place, separating social obstructions and working with a common encounter that rises above contrasts. In friendly settings, whether inside families, companion gatherings, or bigger networks, giggling goes about as a bringing together power that builds up friendly bonds.

Inside the domain of companionship, the language of giggling frequently turns into a shorthand for shared encounters and inside jokes. The capacity to comprehend and partake in one another's humor is a demonstration of the profundity of a relationship, as chuckling turns into a common language that goes beyond anything that can be described. In a work setting, humor and chuckling can act as an incredible asset for group building, diffusing pressure, and cultivating a positive and cooperative climate.

Social Development of Humor:

The development of humor and chuckling mirrors the changing elements of social orders over the long haul. Humor, profoundly implanted in social settings, adjusts to cultural movements, mechanical progressions, and evolving standards.

The language of chuckling, as communicated through humor, turns into a verifiable and social curio, offering bits of knowledge into the aggregate mind of a general public.

Think about the advancement of humor with regards to parody. From old ironical works to current types of political parody in media, humor has been a device for cultural study and discourse. The language of giggling, communicated through parody, adjusts to the subtleties of every time, giving a preview of the overarching social, political, and social issues.

Comprehensive Nature of Chuckling:

One of the momentous characteristics of the language of chuckling is its inclusivity. Giggling has the ability to rise above language boundaries, permitting individuals from various etymological foundations to share snapshots of happiness and entertainment. A common chuckle between people who may not share a typical language turns into a demonstration of the widespread idea of this expressive language.

In a globalized world, where various societies converge, culturally diverse satire fills in as a great representation of the comprehensive idea of giggling. Comics who explore different social settings, as Hasan Minhaj or Ali Wong, use humor that reverberates with crowds independent of their social foundations. The language of chuckling, in these occasions, turns into a scaffold that interfaces individuals through shared comedic encounters.

Giggling in the Computerized Age:

The approach of the computerized age has changed the scene of the language of chuckling. Online entertainment stages, images, and viral recordings have become conductors for the quick scattering of humor across the globe. Images, specifically, address an extraordinary type of visual humor that rises above semantic obstructions, depending on shared social references and viewable signals.

The language of chuckling in the advanced age is described by its promptness and democratization. Anybody with a web association can partake in the creation and dispersal of comical substance, adding to a worldwide embroidery of giggling. Computerized stages act as virtual satire clubs, where people from different foundations can take part in the common language of chuckling, encouraging a feeling of local area in the computerized domain.

Challenges in Deciphering Humor:

While chuckling has a widespread quality, deciphering humor starting with one social setting then onto the next presents extraordinary difficulties. What might be loudly entertaining in one culture might crash and burn or even be seen as hostile in another. The social subtleties implanted in humor, including wit, social references, and normal practices, can present hindrances to powerful multifaceted interpretation.

Comedic subtleties that depend on unambiguous social references or etymological nuances may not interpret consistently. Humor frequently draws on shared social encounters and references, making it setting subordinate. Jokesters acting in assorted social settings frequently wrestle with the test of fitting their humor to reverberate with nearby crowds while keeping up with validness.

The Remedial Force of Chuckling:

Past its social and social aspects, chuckling has helpful characteristics that add to mental and profound prosperity. The field of giggling treatment, or chuckling yoga, has arisen as an organized way to deal with bridling the mending force of chuckling. Giggling yoga meetings include purposeful chuckling practices joined with yogic breathing strategies, advancing unwinding, stress decrease, and a general feeling of prosperity.

The restorative part of chuckling lines up with its antiquated roots in customary medication rehearses. Humor and chuckling were perceived in antiquated societies, including those of the Greeks and Romans, as helpful to physical and emotional wellness. The language of giggling, in this helpful setting, turns into a device for advancing all encompassing wellbeing and strength.

Chuckling and Versatility:

The language of chuckling assumes an essential part in strength, offering people a survival technique to explore life's difficulties and misfortunes. Chuckling, as a reaction to stretch, can give a brief relief from challenges and add to close to home versatility. The capacity to find humor even in tough spots turns into a type of mental strength, permitting people to keep an uplifting perspective notwithstanding difficulty.

In the domain of brain research, Viktor Frankl, the eminent specialist and Holocaust survivor, recognized the significance of humor and giggling as devices for mental endurance. Frankl's perceptions highlighted the job of humor in keeping a feeling of humankind and trust even in the direst conditions. The language of chuckling, in this specific situation, turns into a signal of strength that rises above individual difficulties.

5.1 Playing with Words

Playing with words, an etymological and inventive undertaking, is a sign of mind, humor, and phonetic expertise. Language, being a flexible device, permits people to control words, expressions, and sentence structure to make quips, wit, and cunning articulations that inspire giggling and draw in the psyche. This investigation dives into the specialty of playing with words, looking at its different structures, social aspects, and the intrinsic bliss that emerges from semantic tumbling.

Types of Wit:

Wit includes a heap of structures, each exhibiting the flexibility of language. Quips, homophones, re-arranged words, and risqué statements are only a couple of instances of the different methods utilized in playing with words. Jokes, specifically, include taking advantage of the numerous implications or hints of a word to make a diverting impact. They act as semantic riddles that stimulate the keenness and frequently depend on the interaction of language's polysemous nature.

For example, think about the exemplary joke: "I used to be a cook since I massaged batter." The humor emerges from the risqué remark of "worked," which can mean both the actual activity of plying mixture and the homophonic likeness to "required." This semantic energy adds a layer of shrewdness to the assertion, evoking both entertainment and appreciation for the pleasantry.

Social Components of Pleasantry:

Wit is profoundly implanted in social settings, reflecting semantic customs, colloquial articulations, and authentic subtleties. Various societies have extraordinary ways to deal with playing with words, drawing on the extravagance of their dialects to make humor and convey meaning. Social pleasantry frequently includes quips or phonetic developments that are intended for a specific language or locale.

In Chinese culture, for instance, wit is an esteemed type of articulation. The Mandarin language, with its apparent nature and broad homophones, gives sufficient chances to etymological aerobatic exhibition. Conventional Chinese wit, known as "xiàngshì" (◇◇) or "punning," includes making quips and shrewd word affiliations, frequently consolidating visual components to improve the energy. This social component of pleasantry features its flexibility to the phonetic qualities of a given society.

Semantic Imagination and Mind:

Playing with words is a demonstration of semantic imagination and mind. The capacity to control language, whether through astute jokes, imaginative representations, or perky stating, features a singular's order of language and their ability for innovative articulation. Wit isn't just a phonetic activity; it is a show of scholarly nimbleness and the delight got from etymological resourcefulness.

Oscar Wilde, an expert of mind and wit, exemplified the craft of semantic imagination in his works. His plays and compositions are imbued with sharp repartees, conundrums, and risqué statements that feature his sharp acumen as well as his profound appreciation for the excellence of language. Wilde's popular jest, "I can oppose everything with the exception of enticement," is a great representation of how wit can lift language to a fine art, at the same time conveying humor and knowledge.

Humor in Language:

Humor and language share a natural association, with wit filling in as a strong vehicle for evoking giggling. The unexpected innate in a cunning manner of expression or a startling quip makes a snapshot of mental pleasure, setting off giggling as an unconstrained reaction. The intrinsic bliss in understanding semantic cunning adds an additional layer to the entertainment, making pleasantry a wellspring of both scholarly and close to home delight.

The humor in language frequently lies in the unforeseen associations produced through wit. Whether it's a very much created joke, an etymological turn, or a play on colloquial articulations, the component of shock assumes a vital part in producing giggling. Humorists, authors, and scholars influence this unexpected component to make jokes and articulations that stimulate the amusing bone and make a permanent imprint on the crowd.

Artistic Wit:

Writing, with its extensive material, gives fruitful ground to unpredictable and layered pleasantry. Creators from the beginning of time have utilized wit to improve the profundity and intricacy of their works.

From Shakespeare's quip loaded plays to James Joyce's semantic trials in "Finnegans Wake," scholarly wit adds a component of extravagance to the composed word.

Lewis Carroll's "Alice's Experiences in Wonderland" is an exemplary illustration of scholarly wit. The capricious and fantastical world he made permitted Carroll to play with language in creative ways. The popular sonnet "Jabberwocky" is a superb outline of Carroll's phonetic imagination, as he concocts outlandish words that bring out a striking and perky symbolism. Scholarly wit, in this unique circumstance, turns into a method for mixing the story with a feeling of miracle and phonetic fun loving nature.

Social Analysis through Wit:

Wit isn't restricted to the domain of diversion; it likewise fills in as a device for social discourse. Mocking wit, specifically, includes utilizing language to study cultural standards, parody authority figures, and feature the idiocies of human way of behaving. By playing with words, comedians can pass on complex messages with a portion of humor, making their studies more tasteful and locking in.

Crafted by comedians like Jonathan Quick feature how wit can be employed as a sharp instrument for social investigate. In "Gulliver's Movements," Quick utilizes semantic imagination to parody political and social foundations. The made up lands visited by Gulliver act as moral stories, permitting Quick to play with words to uncover the imprudences and indecencies of contemporary society. Wit, in this specific situation, turns into a method for undermining standards and inciting thought.

Social Wit in Ordinary Language:

In ordinary language, social wit frequently appears in figures of speech, everyday articulations, and local phonetic eccentricities. These phonetic nuances add to the lavishness of correspondence, permitting people to play with words in manners that mirror their social character. Maxims, jokes, and etymological turns become woven into the texture of regular discussions, adding layers of significance and humor.

Think about the English figure of speech "die," significance to pass on. The beginning of this expression is indistinct, yet its utilization as a doublespeak for death adds a hint of levity to a serious subject. Social wit, even in colloquial articulations, mirrors the human propensity to utilize language imaginatively, imbuing ordinary correspondence with subtleties that go past simple strict implications.

Mental Advantages of Wit:

Taking part in pleasantry offers mental advantages past the domain of amusement. The psychological tumbling expected to interpret jokes, re-arranged words, and phonetic questions invigorate mental adaptability and semantic handling. The mind's capacity to explore the layers of significance in wit practices mental capabilities connected with imagination, critical thinking, and etymological understanding.

Pleasantry likewise improves etymological smoothness, extending jargon and encouraging a more profound comprehension of language structures. The energetic control of words urges people to investigate the complexities of language, whether through jokes, re-arranged words, or phonetic riddles. Therefore, pleasantry turns into a mental exercise that advances etymological keenness and mental dexterity.

1. **Double Entendre**

   Risqué remark, an etymological gadget saturated with mind and uncertainty, is a type of wit that adds layers of importance to language. This scholarly and logical strategy includes an expression or articulation that conveys a two sided connotation, frequently one being self-evident and the other more unpretentious or naughty. The actual term, beginning from French, means "two sided connotation," and it fills in as a semantic fine art that flourishes with the sharp utilization of language. This investigation dives into the complexities of risqué statement, looking at its authentic roots, its pervasiveness in writing and regular language, and the nuanced manners by which it explores the territory among blamelessness and interestingness.

Authentic Underlying foundations of Risqué remark:

The underlying foundations of risqué statement can be followed back to old style writing and antiquated way of talking, where talented speakers would utilize phonetic vagueness to convey layered implications. The utilization of risqué statement was not exclusively for comedic impact yet frequently filled in as a device for passing on messages that expected nuance or deniability. Old Greek and Roman writing, with its rich custom of mind and pleasantry, established the groundwork for the development of risqué remark as an explanatory gadget.

In middle age writing, especially during the Renaissance, risqué remark tracked down a home in works of parody and off color humor. Writers like William Shakespeare delighted in the utilization of this phonetic gadget, integrating it into his comedies to draw in crowds in a dance of twofold implications. The allusions and pleasantry in works like "Twelfth Evening" and "A fundamentally nonsensical uproar" exhibited Shakespeare's dominance of language and his capacity to explore the fragile harmony among humor and idea.

Artistic Articulations of Risqué statement:

The domain of writing, with its ability for subtlety and intricacy, gives ripe ground to the investigation of risqué statement. Authors across classes and time spans have utilized this etymological gadget to inject their works with nuance, incongruity, and humor. Frequently, the viability of risqué statement lies in its capacity to connect with perusers in unraveling the double implications implanted in the text.

In the eighteenth hundred years, the plays of French dramatist Molière, for example, "Fraud," highlighted risqué remark as a focal component of comedic discourse. Molière's plays frequently ridiculed cultural standards and lip service, and the sharp wit added a layer of refinement to the humor. Also, the Rebuilding satire in Britain, with writers like William Congreve, delighted in the utilization of risqué remark to make clever and physically interesting chitchat among characters.

In more contemporary writing, writers like James Joyce in "Ulysses" or Vladimir Nabokov in "Lolita" utilized risqué statement to investigate subjects that expected a fragile touch. These works grandstand how this phonetic gadget can be a vehicle for conveying complex feelings, cultural investigates, or mental subtleties.

Regular Language and Mainstream society:

While well established in scholarly customs, risqué remark isn't bound to the domain of highbrow writing. It saturates regular language, tracking down articulation in jokes, promoting, and mainstream society. Comics, publicizing marketing specialists, and lyricists frequently outfit the force of risqué statement to catch consideration, bring out chuckling, and have an enduring impression.

In stand-up parody, entertainers like Richard Pryor or Joan Streams capably utilized risqué statement to handle untouchable subjects with a mix of mind and disrespectfulness. The humor got from risqué statement in satire frequently comes from the pressure between the obvious and secret implications, making a feeling of shock and pleasure for the crowd.

Promoting, with its need to catch consideration and have an enduring effect, oftentimes utilizes risqué statement to pass on messages with a perky edge. Promoters astutely play with words to summon interest, make paramount mottos, and create whiz around items or administrations. The intriguing yet unobtrusive nature of risqué remark in publicizing adds a component of complexity that can resound with different crowds.

In music, tune verses every now and again consolidate risqué statement to convey feelings, recount stories, or investigate subjects that may be considered naughty. Specialists like Sovereign, known for his provocative and exotic verses, frequently utilized risqué remark to inject his melodies with layers of importance.

The transaction among guiltlessness and intriguingness in these verses adds to the appeal of the music and draws in audience members on various levels.

Exploring the Fragile Equilibrium:

The specialty of utilizing risqué remark requires a sensitive harmony among lucidity and equivocalness, idea and limitation. Accomplishing this equilibrium is vital, as going excessively far in either course can bring about a deficiency of effect or, on the other hand, crossing into the domain of obscenity. Talented utilization of risqué statement requires a comprehension of crowd assumptions, social awarenesses, and the setting where the phonetic gadget is utilized.

The parody of risqué remark frequently depends on undermining assumptions, astounding the crowd, and evoking giggling through the disclosure of profound implications. Nonetheless, this type of humor isn't without its difficulties, as what one finds entertaining, another could view as hostile. The emotional idea of humor and the potential for distortion highlight the requirement for a nuanced and smart methodology while utilizing risqué remark in any type of correspondence.

Social Varieties in Risqué statement:

Social standards and restrictions essentially impact the discernment and acknowledgment of risqué remark. What might be viewed as fun loving and clever in one culture may be considered unseemly or hostile in another. Understanding the social subtleties and responsive qualities encompassing risqué remark is critical, particularly in a globalized reality where correspondence rises above borders.

In certain societies, there might be a more noteworthy capacity to bear perky and interesting language, while in others, a more safe methodology might be normal. The progress of risqué remark in exploring these social varieties lies in its capacity to convey layered implications without causing uneasiness or disregarding cultural standards.

Moral Contemplations:

While risqué remark can be an amazing asset for imaginative articulation, it isn't without moral contemplations. The potential for confusion, particularly in settings where power elements or touchy subjects are impacting everything, highlights the requirement for cautious thought and mindful utilization of this phonetic gadget.

In the domain of humor, jokesters frequently wrestle with the barely recognizable difference among restless and hostile substance. The effect of risqué remark can change broadly contingent upon the social, social, and authentic setting in which it is introduced. Comics and content makers should be receptive to the likely outcomes of their words, perceiving that humor can affect people and networks.

2. **Innuendo**

Insinuation, an inconspicuous and frequently intriguing type of articulation, winds through the texture of language, adding a layer of intricacy to correspondence. Gotten from the Italian word "innuere," signifying "to gesture to" or "to imply," insinuation includes hidden implications, intimations, or roundabout references that welcome the crowd to find out a deeper meaning. This investigation dives into the subtleties of allusion, analyzing its authentic roots, its part in writing and ordinary discussion, and the shrewd dance it performs between the plain and the secret.

Verifiable Underlying foundations of Allusion:

The underlying foundations of insinuation can be followed back to antiquated expository customs, where speakers and authors used hidden language to pass on messages that necessary nuance or deniability. In old style writing, especially in works from old Greece and Rome, insinuation frequently filled in as a device for communicating feelings or evaluates that might have been considered unseemly or questionable.

The Renaissance period saw a prospering of insinuation in writing, with essayists like William Shakespeare excelling at hidden language. Plays, for example, "Romeo and Juliet" and "A fundamentally nonsensical uproar" are loaded with occasions where characters utilize insinuation to convey profound implications, adding layers of intricacy to the exchange. This verifiable point of reference laid out insinuation as a complex and nuanced type of articulation that rises above time and social movements.

Scholarly Investigation of Allusion:

In writing, allusion turns into a strong story gadget, permitting writers to convey complex feelings, cultural scrutinizes, or mental subtleties without expressly expressing them. This type of circuitous correspondence connects with perusers in a dance of translation, welcoming them to unravel profound implications and unobtrusive suggestions.

In progress of Jane Austen, insinuation assumes an essential part in portraying the social complexities and heartfelt strains of the characters. In "Pride and Bias," for instance, the chitchat between Elizabeth Bennet and Mr. Darcy is weighed down with allusion, making a propensity of importance underneath the outer layer of more polite circles. Austen's utilization of hidden language adds profundity to the social editorial woven into her books.

James Joyce, in his original work "Ulysses," utilizes allusion to investigate the mental intricacies of his characters. The continuous flow story style permits Joyce to dive into the inward contemplations and wants of the characters through unobtrusive clues and inferences, making a rich embroidery of implying that requires dynamic peruser commitment.

Regular Language and Conversational Subtleties:

Past the domains of writing, insinuation is an unavoidable component of ordinary language, molding discussions and social connections. It works in different structures, from energetic prodding and tease to additional serious and unpretentious ramifications. In group environments, allusion turns into a device for communicating feelings that might be awkward or unseemly to straightforwardly expressive.

In easygoing chat, companions might take part in insinuation as a type of happy prodding or to convey lively goals. The intriguing idea of insinuation frequently presents a component of humor and makes a mutual perspective among members. In additional serious discussions, allusion might be utilized to address fragile subjects or propose delicate points with a level of prudence.

The working environment is another field where insinuation can assume a part, once in a while straying into the domain of workplace issues or unpretentious power elements. The utilization of hidden language in proficient settings might include roundabout studies, stowed away plans, or vital correspondence that requires cautious translation by those included.

Humor and Allusion:

In the domain of humor, allusion becomes the dominant focal point, adding a bit of ribald or intriguing liveliness to jokes and comedic exhibitions. Joke artists frequently use insinuation to draw in their crowds, depending on the common perspective that accompanies unpretentious ramifications and profound implications. The humor got from insinuation frequently relies on the strain between the obvious and the clandestine, making a feeling of shock and entertainment.

Professional comics like Mae West or Groucho Marx were known for their proficient utilization of allusion, pushing the limits of cultural standards and utilizing hidden language to incite giggling. The shrewd sending of interesting language turned into a sign of their comedic style, testing social restrictions and charming crowds with sharp wit.

Exploring the Limits:

While insinuation can be a complex and powerful type of correspondence, it likewise explores fragile limits, particularly in contemporary settings where aversions to language and suggestions have developed. The barely recognizable difference between fun loving prodding and unseemly hints requires a sharp familiarity with social elements, social standards, and the solace levels of those included.

In the period of elevated mindfulness around issues of assent and deferential correspondence, the utilization of allusion requests a smart and circumspect methodology. What might be considered clever or satisfactory in one setting could be seen as hostile or unseemly in another. Exploring these limits includes an acknowledgment of the power elements at play and a comprehension of the likely effect of hidden language on different crowds.

Social Varieties in Allusion:

Social standards altogether impact the translation and agreeableness of allusion. What might be viewed as clever and adequate in one culture may be considered rough or hostile in another. The social varieties in the utilization of hidden language feature the requirement for awareness and social ability in correspondence.

In certain societies, allusion might be embraced as a characteristic and lively part of correspondence, while in others, a more straightforward and express methodology might be leaned toward. Understanding the social subtleties encompassing allusion is fundamental, particularly in assorted and multicultural settings where translations might contrast in light of individual and aggregate encounters.

Moral Contemplations in Allusion:

Allusion, when utilized recklessly, can have moral ramifications, especially in circumstances where power elements, assent, or expert connections become possibly the most important factor. The potential for mistaken assumptions or misinterpretations highlights the significance of moral contemplations while utilizing hidden language, whether in private communications or expert settings.

In the time of expanded consciousness of working environment elements, conversations around assent, and the significance of clear correspondence, people should explore allusion with an uplifted feeling of obligation. Being aware of the effect of hidden language on others and taking into account the expected outcomes of distortion is vital for moral correspondence.

5.2 Embracing Absurdity

Embracing idiocy, a philosophical and inventive position, welcomes people to face the innate inconsistencies, disjointed qualities, and madnesses of presence with humor and acknowledgment. Established in existentialist idea and advocated by scholars like Albert Camus and Franz Kafka, the idea of ludicrousness challenges ordinary thoughts of importance and reason. This investigation digs into the multi-layered nature of embracing craziness, looking at its philosophical underpinnings, its sign in writing and craftsmanship, and its extraordinary power as a focal point through which to see the human experience.

Philosophical Underpinnings of Ridiculousness:

The philosophical investigation of ridiculousness tracks down its underlying foundations in existentialism, a philosophical development that wrestles with the human condition, opportunity, and the journey for significance. Albert Camus, in his original article "The Fantasy of Sisyphus," investigates the possibility of the crazy as the contention between the human craving for significance and the evident triviality of the universe.

Sisyphus, sentenced by the divine beings to move a stone up a slope just to see it roll down forever, turns into the existential prime example. Camus battles that Sisyphus, notwithstanding his apparently worthless and silly errand, can track down importance and reason through his cognizant decision to embrace the craziness of his issue. Even with a universe without any trace of innate significance, people, as indicated by Camus, have the ability to oppose despair and make their own importance through cognizant, silly living.

Abstract Signs of Craziness:

Writing has been a fruitful ground for the investigation of ludicrousness, with writers like Franz Kafka, Samuel Beckett, and Kurt Vonnegut embracing the silly as a topical foundation. Kafka's "The Transformation" acquaints perusers with Gregor Samsa, who gets up one morning changed into a goliath bug. The silliness of this transformation fills in as a similitude for the peculiar and erratic nature of presence.

Essentially, Samuel Beckett's play "Sitting tight for Godot" exemplifies the silly by including two characters, Vladimir and Estragon, perpetually sitting tight for somebody named Godot who won't ever show up. The play's round and apparently unimportant design catches the substance of silliness, provoking the crowd to scrutinize the motivation behind pausing and the idea of presence.

Kurt Vonnegut, in works like "Slaughterhouse-Five," utilizes craziness to investigate the effect of battle on human awareness. The hero, Billy Explorer, becomes "unstuck in time," encountering occasions in a nonlinear design. This account structure reflects the disconnected and turbulent nature of war, underlining the silliness innate in endeavors to figure out the silly.

Creative Articulations of Idiocy:

Past writing, the hug of silliness saturates the domain of visual expressions. The Surrealist development, with craftsmen like Salvador Dalí and René Magritte, embraced the silly and the illogical for the purpose of testing cultural standards and investigating the openings of the oblivious psyche.

Dalí's notorious painting, "The Ingenuity of Memory," highlights dissolving clocks hung over desolate scenes, causing a strange and fanciful situation. The contorted and melted clocks represent the relativity of time and the moldable idea of the real world. Magritte, known for his mysterious and provocative works, challenges ordinary insights with pieces like "The Unfairness of Pictures," which portrays a line with the subtitle "Ceci n'est pas une pipe" (This isn't a line). This play on portrayal and language exemplifies the silliness of images and their relationship to the real world.

Humor and Idiocy:

Embracing idiocy frequently includes a significant funny bone — an acknowledgment of the entertaining and silly parts of life. The ludicrous and the hilarious offer a harmonious relationship, with humor filling in as a survival technique notwithstanding life's inborn inconsistencies. Joke artists, from the mind of Monty Python to the contemptuousness of absurdist stand-up, influence craziness to incite giggling while at the same time provoking reflection on the ludicrousness of human life.

The humor of idiocy frequently lies in the surprising and the counter-intuitive. Comedic outlines, similar to those of the Marx Siblings or the craziness of "The Drifter's Manual for the Universe" by Douglas Adams, revel in circumstances and exchanges that oppose objectivity. The chuckling that follows isn't only a getaway yet a type of disobedience to the gravity of presence — a festival of the ridiculousness that highlights the human experience.

Extraordinary Force of Ludicrousness:

Embracing idiocy can be an extraordinary and freeing experience. By recognizing the innate madnesses of life, people might liberate themselves from the weights of a quest for extreme importance and reason. All things considered, the center movements to the quick, the substantial, and the experiential — an acknowledgment that significance can be tracked down in the demonstration of living itself.

This groundbreaking power is clear in the idea of "existential legitimacy," where people, by embracing the silliness of presence, defy their own opportunity to make meaning. This idea lines up with existentialist masterminds like Jean-Paul Sartre, who contended that people are sentenced to be free and should assume a sense of ownership with their decisions. The acknowledgment of idiocy turns into a passage to real living — a cognizant commitment with one's presence without surrendering to skepticism.

Difficulties and Versatility:

While embracing craziness offers freedom, it isn't without challenges. Exploring the silly requires a fragile harmony among acknowledgment and a proactive commitment with life. The peril lies in surrendering to disregard or skepticism, where the affirmation of ridiculousness turns into a support for lack of concern.

Flexibility despite the crazy includes developing a feeling of organization — an eagerness to defy life's vulnerabilities with imagination and reason. Camus' thought of "revolt" against the silly urges people to defy despair and, in doing as such, to develop their own importance. This flexibility isn't a disavowal of the ridiculous however a gutsy reaction to it — an insistence of life in spite of its intrinsic inconsistencies.

1. **Surreal Humor**

Strange humor, a sort that opposes customary comedic shows, welcomes crowds into a domain where the standard is overturned, rationale is suspended, and the ridiculous rules. Established in the Surrealist development that arose in the mid twentieth hundred years, strange humor disturbs natural examples of thought, testing assumptions and making a space where the irrational turns into a wellspring of giggling. This investigation digs into the starting points of dreamlike humor, its sign in different types of diversion, and the novel allure of this sort in offering a great break from the limitations of the real world.

Beginnings in Oddity:

Strange humor tracks down its foundations in Oddity, a vanguard creative and artistic development that arose in the fallout of The Second Great War. Driven by figures like André Breton, Salvador Dalí, and René Magritte, Oddity tried to open the innovative capability of the oblivious psyche, freeing workmanship from the requirements of reason and objectivity. The development's impact reached out past visual expressions and writing, saturating into the domain of humor and satire.

André Breton, the pioneer behind Oddity, had faith in the force of humor to disturb cultural standards and challenge traditional reasoning. Surrealist craftsmen frequently integrated unusual and fanciful components into their works, dismissing the limitations of direct accounts and welcoming watchers to investigate the unreasonable and fantastical.

Sign in Writing and Film:

In writing, strange humor found articulation through crafted by writers like Lewis Carroll, Franz Kafka, and later, in the ludicrous plays of Eugène Ionesco and Samuel Beckett.

Lewis Carroll's "Alice's Experiences in Wonderland" takes perusers on an eccentric excursion through a reality where rationale is undermined, and characters participate in crazy discussions and exercises. Kafka's "The Transformation" acquaints perusers with the strange reason of a man awakening to wind up changed into a goliath bug, testing ideas of the real world and character.

In the domain of movie, chiefs like Luis Buñuel and David Lynch embraced oddity, implanting their works with fanciful groupings and strange accounts. Buñuel's "Un Chien Andalou" broadly opens with a famous picture of a razor cutting through an eyeball, establishing the vibe for a film that resists conventional narrating. David Lynch, known for works like "Mulholland Drive" and "Twin Pinnacles," makes dreamlike scenes where the limits among dreams and reality obscure, agitating crowds with the unforeseen and the baffling.

TV and Sketch Satire:

Strange humor tracked down a characteristic home in TV, especially in sketch satire. Shows like "Monty Python's Flying Carnival" became notorious for their disrespectful and silly portrayals. The Pythons, including John Cleese, Eric Inactive, and Michael Palin, made portrays that resisted customary zingers and account structures. From the "Dead Parrot Sketch" to the "Service of Senseless Strolls," Monty Python's humor embraced the dreamlike, provoking watchers to draw in with the surprising and the crazy.

Essentially, the American sketch satire show "The Children in the Lobby" exhibited a strange and unpredictable way to deal with humor. The group, comprising of Dave Foley, Kevin McDonald, Bruce McCulloch, Imprint McKinney, and Scott Thompson, mixed silly characters and circumstances with a novel blend of mind and social discourse. Their representations frequently wandered into the dreamlike, making an unmistakable comedic style.

Liveliness and Strange Satire:

The enlivened domain has likewise been a fruitful ground for strange humor. Illustrators and makers have utilized the boundless conceivable outcomes of liveliness to create universes where the laws of physical science and the truth are energetically disposed of. "The Simpsons," for instance, frequently integrates strange components into its story, with episodes including fantastical situations and dream groupings.

Grown-up Swim, a late-evening programming block on Animation Organization, has been a trailblazer in displaying vivified series that embrace strange and offbeat humor. "Water High schooler Craving Power" and "Rick and Morty" both investigate the craziness of presence through fantastical plots, peculiar characters, and an eagerness to undermine story assumptions.

Idiocy and Social Analysis:

Strange humor, while savoring the experience of the outlandish, frequently fills in as a vehicle for social and political discourse. By upsetting recognizable standards and shows, dreamlike comics and makers can cause to notice the idiocies of contemporary life. This type of humor turns into an instrument for ridiculing cultural designs, addressing authority, and rocking the boat.

Crafted by English comic Chris Morris, especially the TV series "Metal Eye," represent this crossing point of idiocy and social investigate. "Metal Eye" utilizes a mockumentary organization to ridicule media emotionalism and public guilelessness. By taking on a dreamlike focal point, Morris uncovered the ludicrousness of media stories and the manners by which falsehood can shape public insight.

Crowd Commitment and the Erratic:

The allure of strange humor lies in its capacity to astound and connect with crowds in the flighty. Dissimilar to customary parody, which frequently follows laid out designs of arrangement and zinger, dreamlike humor revels in the startling and the capricious. Watchers and crowds are urged to give up the requirement for intelligence and direct account, embracing the disorder and arbitrariness of the comedic experience.

This unusualness encourages a functioning commitment with the material, as crowds should explore the counter-intuitive and figure out the irrational. In doing as such, strange humor turns into a participatory encounter, welcoming watchers to find their own translations and implications inside the silliness introduced.

2. Nonsensical Comedy

Strange parody, an eccentric and ludicrous sort of humor, revels in the irrational, the ridiculous, and the out and out senseless. It fills in as a superb takeoff from the imperatives of soundness, embracing an existence where the garbled rules. This investigation dives into the beginnings of illogical satire, its appearances in writing, film, and execution, and the novel allure of humor that makes no sense and delights in the counter-intuitive.

Establishes in Gibberish Writing:

Counter-intuitive parody has its foundations in the rich custom of gibberish writing that arose in the nineteenth hundred years. Spearheaded by writers like Lewis Carroll and Edward Lear, this type looked to charm perusers with energetic language, ludicrous situations, and eccentric characters. Lewis Carroll's "Alice's Experiences in Wonderland" and "Into another world" transport perusers to universes where rationale is undermined, and the silly turns into the standard. The Distraught Hatter's casual get-together and the Cheshire Feline's puzzling smile typify the impulsive notion and silliness that characterize illogical satire.

Edward Lear, known for his limericks and abstract garbage, made fantastical scenes and animals in works like "The Owl and the Pussycat." The purposeful utilization of fun loving language and the shortfall of clear significance describe these silly refrains, welcoming perusers to delight in phonetic idiocy.

Oddity and Dadaism:

Outlandish parody tracked down connection with the Surrealist and Dada developments of the mid twentieth 100 years. Surrealist specialists like Salvador Dalí and René Magritte embraced the ludicrous and the unreasonable in their visual works, testing regular ideas of the real world. Dadaists, including Marcel Duchamp, tried to upset cultural standards through demonstrations of irregularity and idiocy. These developments impacted the development of counter-intuitive satire, adding to its rise as a particular comedic classification.

Abstract Hogwash in the twentieth 100 years:

During the twentieth 100 years, the class encountered a resurgence with crafted by scholars like Dr. Seuss (Theodor Seuss Geisel) and Roald Dahl. Dr. Seuss' unusual stories, including "The Feline in the Cap" and "Green Eggs and Ham," charmed youngsters and grown-ups the same with their energetic language and unreasonable situations. His dominance of wit and the making of fantastical universes laid out him as a vital figure in silly writing.

Roald Dahl, referred to for books, for example, "Charlie and the Chocolate Plant" and "The BFG," mixed his narrating with a mix of silliness and incorrigible humor. The eccentric characters and impossible to miss occasions in Dahl's works add to the feeling of the counter-intuitive, making an extraordinary mix of imagination and humor.

Film and TV:

Illogical satire tracked down a characteristic home in film and TV, where visual and performative components upgrade its ridiculousness. The Marx Siblings, in films like "No brainer" and "A Night at the Show," utilized a style of humor portrayed by quick fire wit, dream-like situations, and crazy shenanigans. Groucho Marx's clever jokes and Harpo Marx's quiet, actual satire typified the illogical on the cinema.

Monty Python, the English satire group, advanced the tradition of irrational parody in the TV series "Monty Python's Flying Bazaar." Representations like "The Service of Senseless Strolls" and "The Spanish

Probe" embraced the crazy, testing account shows and stimulating the crowd's entertaining bone with sheer nonsensicality.

Stand-Up Satire and Comedy:

In the domain of stand-up satire, entertainers like Andy Kaufman and Steven Wright embraced a style that opposed customary zingers and story cognizance.

Andy Kaufman's vanguard approach, described by whimsical characters and hostile to go along with, obscured the lines between execution workmanship and parody. Steven Wright's empty conveyance and silly perceptions added to the advancement of irrational humor in stand-up.

Improvisational parody, especially as comedy theater, frequently integrates outlandish components. The suddenness of comedy permits entertainers to embrace the unforeseen, causing situations and characters that make no sense and revel in the silly. Comedy bunches like The Groundlings and Second City have developed a practice of unreasonable satire in front of an audience.

The Ludicrous Allure:

The remarkable allure of counter-intuitive satire lies in its capacity to give a break from the levelheaded and the anticipated. In a world frequently overwhelmed by rationale and reason, the irrational fills in as a reviving takeoff, offering crowds an opportunity to escape into a domain where the startling is praised, and the unusual is embraced.

The chuckling got from counter-intuitive satire isn't established in conventional arrangements and zingers however emerges from the sheer delight of seeing the crazy unfurl. The capriciousness, the semantic liveliness, and the surrender of regular designs add to an encounter that rises above the normal.

Irrational Satire as a Social Evaluate:

Past its job as a wellspring of diversion, irrational satire can likewise act as a type of social evaluate. By undermining laid out standards and shows, absurd humor has the ability to challenge cultural assumptions and question the state of affairs. From the perspective of the silly, comics and makers can cause to notice the idiocies of contemporary life and brief crowds to rethink their viewpoints.

6

Chapter 6

Beyond the Punchline

Past the zinger lies an immense and nuanced scene in the domain of satire, where humor rises above the limits of customary arrangements and giggling turns into a complex encounter. This investigation digs into the profundities of comedic craftsmanship, looking at the layers that exist past the zinger — investigating the intricacies of timing, subtext, and the fragile creativity that changes a joke into a noteworthy and significant comedic second.

Timing and Mood:

At the core of comedic splendor lies the dominance of timing — an inconspicuous dance that isolates a decent joke from an incredible one. Understanding when to convey the zinger, considering the ideal delay, or handily exploring the beats of a comedic routine changes humor into a cadenced encounter. The conveyance of a zinger at the exact second can raise a joke, making an expectation that finishes in chuckling. This worldly aspect is a principal part of comedic timing, where the comic goes about as a director organizing the beat of chuckling.

Comedic timing reaches out past the simple conveyance of zingers; it envelops the pacing of a daily schedule, the rhythm of exchange, and the sly control of quietness.

The all around coordinated delay can be basically as significant as the actual zinger, permitting the crowd to ingest the humor and upgrading the comedic impact. The inborn comprehension of this comedic musicality recognizes comics who reverberate profoundly with their crowd, making an encounter that goes past the confined giggling incited by individual jokes.

Subtext and Subtlety:

Past the plain diversion of zingers lies the rich territory of subtext and subtlety — a domain where entertainers create unpretentious layers of importance, social discourse, or ludicrousness underneath the surface. Comedic splendor frequently includes the smart transaction of words and thoughts, where the genuine humor lies in what is said as well as in what is left implied.

Subtextual humor welcomes the crowd to participate in a type of scholarly play, translating profound implications, and unwinding the layers of mind. The rebellious idea of subtext permits comics to explore delicate points, challenge cultural standards, or weave complex stories that reverberate on different levels. This layering of importance changes satire into a complex fine art, welcoming the crowd to become dynamic members in the unwinding of comedic brightness.

Character Elements and Exchange:

In the realm of sitcoms, stand-up schedules, or comedic portrays, the elements between characters assume a critical part in making humor that goes past the zinger. The transaction of characters, the science among entertainers, and the improvement of repeating themes add to the life span and memorability of comedic minutes. It's not just about conveying jokes; about the connections and cooperations unfurl inside the comedic universe.

All around made characters carry profundity and credibility to comedic accounts, permitting the crowd to associate sincerely with the humor. The unconventionalities, peculiarities, and eccentricities of characters become comedic apparatuses, forming the comedic scene and adding to the getting through allure of specific comedies. Whether it's the ageless talk among Lucy and Ethel in "I Love Lucy" or the useless brotherhood of the characters in "It's Generally Bright in Philadelphia," the extravagance of character elements broadens the comedic experience past individual zingers.

Social Setting and Parody:

Parody, at its ideal, fills in as a mirror mirroring the subtleties and idiocies of the social scene. Parody, a type of humor that utilizes incongruity, misrepresentation, or scorn to study and ridicule cultural shows, goes past the zinger to offer a significant editorial on the world. Entertainers who excel at parody explore the fragile equilibrium between humor and social study, involving giggling as an instrument for thoughtfulness and reflection.

The adequacy of ironical satire lies in its capacity to enlighten cultural issues, challenge power structures, and incite smart talk. By drawing in with the social setting, entertainers make material that resounds with crowds on a more profound level, provoking them to consider the more extensive ramifications of the humor introduced. Mocking parody, with its foundations in old practices of political parody, features the getting through force of humor to rise above simple entertainment and become a power for social critique.

Comedy and Immediacy:

The universe of improvisational satire, where entertainers cause situations, characters, and discourse on the spot, epitomizes a type of comedic articulation that goes past prearranged zingers. In comedy, the unforeseen turns into the standard, and the humor rises out of the immediacy existing apart from everything else. The cooperative idea of comedy, where entertainers expand on one another's thoughts, adds a component of capriciousness that keeps crowds locked in.

The excellence of comedy lies in its smoothness, permitting jokesters to investigate unfamiliar comedic domain. The mind showed in answering startling prompts, the consistent consolidation of crowd ideas, and the capacity to explore unscripted situations exhibit a type of comedic creativity that rises above the limits of biased zingers. In the realm of comedy, the excursion becomes as significant as the objective, and the delight of disclosure remains closely connected with the delight of chuckling.

6.1 Crafting Endearing Characters

Making charming characters in narrating is a workmanship that rises above the limits of fiction, making figures that resound with crowds on a significant and profound level. Whether in writing, film, or any story medium, the most common way of building characters includes a fragile mix of characteristics, encounters, and development that changes them from simple plot gadgets into substances that summon sympathy and connection. This investigation digs into the complexities of character making, looking at the components that add to the charming idea of fictitious personas and the effect they have on the general account.

1. **Appeal and Comprehensiveness:**

   Charming characters frequently have characteristics that resound with the widespread human experience, making them interesting to an expansive crowd. Scholars and makers draw on central feelings, battles, and goals that associate people across societies and foundations. Whether it's the quest for adoration, the journey for personality, or the defeating of affliction, characters with appealing encounters become standards so that perusers or watchers might see themselves reflected in the account.

   Appeal stretches out past superficial attributes to include the center of human life. Blemishes, weaknesses, and defects make characters credible, permitting crowds to relate to their battles and praise their victories. In making charming characters, makers explore the harmony among uniqueness and comprehensiveness, guaranteeing that while characters might be unmistakable, their close to home centers remain all around conspicuous.

2. **Profundity and Intricacy:**

   Charming characters are not one-layered; they have profundity and intricacy that unfurl progressively all through the story. Layers of character, inspirations, and struggles under the surface add to a person's wealth, welcoming crowds to participate in a course of disclosure. A person's intricacy frequently reflects the complexities of genuine people, making them really convincing and fascinating.

   The excursion of uncovering a person's profundity can include a cautious investigation of their past, injuries, and developmental encounters. This cycle permits the crowd to grasp the main thrusts behind a person's activities, cultivating a more profound association. The revealing of a person's intricacy frequently makes a feeling of venture, as crowds become sincerely engaged with the unfurling story of the person's life.

3. **Defective Flawlessness:**

   Charming characters are intrinsically defective, having flaws that adapt them and make them engaging. Imperfections add legitimacy to characters, keeping them from becoming glorified or out of reach. It is through characters' defects that crowds observer their versatility, development, and the limit with regards to change, cultivating a feeling of compassion and association.

   The interchange among qualities and shortcomings makes a nuanced representation of a person, permitting crowds to see past superficial characteristics. Blemishes become open doors for characters to learn, develop, and face the difficulties introduced by the story. The excursion of beating defects or embracing them frequently turns into a focal subject in the person's turn of events, adding layers to their charming nature.

4. **Critical Peculiarities and Propensities:**

   Charming characters frequently have noteworthy peculiarities or propensities that recognize them and make them remarkable. These mannerisms add to the person's peculiarity and make snapshots of levity or appeal. Idiosyncrasies can go from curious discourse examples to remarkable signals or even unambiguous interests that put the person aside.

Significant idiosyncrasies act as anchors for crowds, giving standards that upgrade the person's character. At the point when these eccentricities line up with the person's inspirations or foundation, they become strong narrating devices, extending the's comprehension crowd might interpret the person's mind. Idiosyncrasies, when very much created, add to a person's charming heritage, making them hang out in the recollections of crowds.

5. **Developing Connections:**

The manner in which a person explores and adds to connections inside the story fundamentally influences their charming quality. Significant associations with different characters — whether companionships, sentiments, or familial ties — permit crowds to observe the person in unique and true connections. The advancement of these connections gives chances to characters to uncover various features of themselves.

Charming characters frequently evoke sympathy through their own excursions as well as through the bonds they structure with others. The weakness and validness showed in connections make close to home reverberation, as crowds put in the singular characters as well as in the associations that dilemma them. All around made connections add to the person's general affability and charm.

6. **Strength and Development:**

The excursion of a charming person is frequently set apart by strength even with difficulties and significant self-improvement. Conquering difficulty, standing up to fears, and developing because of encounters make a person bend that reverberates with crowds. The story turns into a vessel for displaying the person's groundbreaking process.

The way to creating strength lies in giving characters obstructions that test their cutoff points, pushing them past their usual ranges of familiarity. The continuous movement from weakness to strength cultivates a feeling of deference and love from the crowd. Seeing characters develop and gain from their encounters adds a layer of close to home venture, making their excursion convincing as well as profoundly charming.

7. **Credible Exchange and Voice:**

Charming characters are rejuvenated through credible exchange and a particular story voice. The manner in which a person puts themselves out there — through words, tone, and inward speeches — shapes their character and adds to the crowd's view of them. Genuineness in discourse permits crowds to associate with characters on a close to home and scholarly level.

Making a person's voice includes grasping their character, foundation, and the subtleties of their singular encounters. Whether clever, reflective, or graceful, the validness of a person's voice turns into a scaffold between the imaginary world and the crowd. Very much created exchange improves the generally speaking charming nature of a person by causing them to feel certified and engaging.

1. **Balancing Humor and Heart**

Adjusting humor and heart in narrating is a sensitive workmanship that includes consistently entwining snapshots of giggling with those of veritable inclination. This complicated dance among parody and sincere minutes makes stories that resound profoundly with crowds, evoking both giggling and a significant close to home association. This investigation dives into the subtleties of finding some kind of harmony, looking at how narrators explore the territory among humor and heart to create stories that leave an enduring effect.

1. **Laying out Profound Anchors:**
   At the center of adjusting humor and heart lies the foundation of close to home anchors inside the account. These anchors are snapshots of earnestness, weakness, or certifiable human association that ground the story in an engaging and genuine reality. Whether it's a person's very own battle, an impactful disclosure, or a common snapshot of weakness, these profound anchors give an establishment to the crowd to put genuinely in the story.
   Laying out these anchors from the beginning permits the crowd to frame an association with the characters and the story past the comedic components. The close to home reverberation made by these minutes turns into a reference point, enhancing the generally speaking narrating experience. At the point when humor is layered on this establishment, it acquires profundity and power, making a story embroidery that is both carefree and sincerely resounding.

2. **Character-driven Humor:**
   Successful adjusting of humor and heart frequently originates from character-driven satire. At the point when humor arises naturally from the characteristics, peculiarities, and encounters of advanced characters, it produces chuckles as well as develops the crowd's comprehension and warmth for the characters. The comedic components become an expansion of the's characters, making the humor genuine and necessary to the narrating.
   Character-driven humor depends on the extraordinary characteristics of people inside the account, permitting their comedic minutes to emerge normally from their cooperations and conditions. This approach guarantees that the humor is definitely not a disconnected component forced on the story yet an inherent piece of the characters' lives. Subsequently, the giggling turns out to be more significant, making a connection between the crowd and the characters.

3. **Timing and Pacing:**

   Adjusting humor and heart requires fastidious thoughtfulness regarding timing and pacing. The consistent incorporation of comedic thumps with snapshots of profound weight relies on a comprehension of when to inspire chuckling and when to bring out a sincere reaction. Pacing considers the back and forth movement of feelings, making a story cadence that keeps the crowd connected with and contributed.

   Successful timing guarantees that silly components improve, instead of eclipse, the profound beats of the story. Very much positioned snapshots of levity can give help, increase profound effect, or act as a scaffold between differentiating tones. The dominance of timing and pacing permits narrators to direct the crowd through a rollercoaster of feelings, making a story that feels dynamic and bona fide.

4. **Undermining Assumptions:**

   Adjusting humor and heart frequently includes undermining crowd assumptions. While comedic arrangements might lead watchers down recognizable ways, the story can go off in strange directions that infuse snapshots of strength or thoughtfulness. Alternately, genuine scenes can be intruded on by all around coordinated comedic turns, keeping the crowd honest and keeping the story from becoming unsurprising.

   Undermining assumptions requires a cautious equilibrium to keep away from apparent whiplash. When done really, it adds layers to the narrating, considering a more nuanced investigation of subjects and characters. This approach welcomes crowds to connect all the more profoundly, as they are continued to figure about the heading of the story, making a mix of shock, chuckling, and real inclination.

5. **Investigating Double Real factors:**

   A convincing method for adjusting humor and heart is by investigating double real factors inside the story. This method includes giving characters differentiating points of view or circumstances — one comical and the other ardent — permitting the two components to coincide inside a similar story. This duality gives a nuanced investigation of the human experience, exhibiting the intricacy of feelings.

Double real factors can be depicted through equal storylines, different person viewpoints, or apparent movements inside the account. By comparing humor and heart, narrators make a rich and finished narrating experience. This procedure takes into consideration a more thorough assessment of characters' lives, connections, and self-awareness, guaranteeing that both the comedic and profound perspectives add to the story's general reverberation.

6. **Keeping up with Legitimacy:**

Most importantly, adjusting humor and heart requires a guarantee to realness. The profound beats should sound accurate to the characters and the story's subjects, while the humor ought to emerge naturally from the account's unique situation. Credibility guarantees that the giggling feels procured, and the close to home minutes are true, resounding with crowds on a veritable level.

Keeping up with validness includes figuring out the tone and subjects of the story, as well as remaining consistent with the laid out character elements. Humor ought to be a characteristic outgrowth of the's characters and the circumstances they regard themselves as in, as opposed to constrained or devised. At the point when humor and heart adjust legitimately, the narrating turns into a strong vehicle for interfacing with the crowd on both a scholarly and close to home level.

b. Character Development in Comedy

Character improvement in parody is a nuanced and fundamental part of narrating that rises above the simple quest for chuckles. While humor frames the foundation of comedic stories, very much created characters assume a significant part in lifting the comedic experience, making a unique transaction between mind, character, and development. This investigation dives into the complexities of character improvement in parody, looking at how the advancement of characters adds to the wealth of comedic narrating.

1. **Prologue to Models:**

   Comedic accounts frequently start by presenting characters established in unmistakable paradigms or generalizations. These models act as natural layouts, giving a beginning stage to comedic investigation. Whether it's the blundering companion, the serious hero, or the clever pessimist, paradigms establish the groundwork for comedic elements. Be that as it may, the enchantment of character improvement in parody lies in undermining these models, adding profundity, and resisting assumptions.

2. **Laying out One of a kind Characters:**

   While models offer a beginning stage, the course of character improvement includes figuring out extraordinary characters that go past shallow generalizations. Advanced comedic characters have particular characteristics, eccentricities, and mannerisms that make them paramount. These attributes become comedic instruments, forming the person's associations, reactions, and the humor that emerges from their unmistakable perspective.

   The foundation of one of a kind characters makes way for character-driven humor, where the giggling arises naturally from the characters' qualities and the circumstances they explore. Whether it's the flighty neighbor with a liking for unconventional side interests or the mocking closest companion with an inclination for clever rebounds, the particularity of character qualities turns into a wellspring of comedic potential.

3. **Change and Development:**

   Character improvement in satire isn't static; it includes a course of change and development. As characters explore the comedic exciting bends in the road of the story, they go through changes that add to the generally comedic circular segment.

The development of characters might include defeating individual defects, standing up to silly difficulties, or adjusting to unforeseen circumstances, making a dynamic and connecting with comedic venture.

The way to fruitful person development in satire is keeping a sensitive harmony among change and consistency. While characters advance, their fundamental qualities and idiosyncrasies stay in salvageable shape, guaranteeing that the humor remains established in the legitimacy of their characters. This equilibrium permits crowds to put resources into the characters' excursions while partaking in the comedic coherence that emerges from their center credits.

4. **The Force of Weakness:**

One of the most strong components of character advancement in satire is the investigation of weakness. Satire frequently flourishes with uncovering the instabilities, fears, and weaknesses of characters, making snapshots of certified humankind in the midst of the chuckling. The crowd's capacity to understand characters' weaknesses encourages a more profound association, changing comedic minutes into sincerely thunderous encounters.

Weakness in parody can appear in different structures, from the hero confronting humiliating circumstances to the disclosure of a person's feelings of trepidation or goals. At the point when characters uncover their weaknesses, it acculturates them, making them engaging and charming. This human association turns into an amazing asset for evoking giggling that isn't just entertaining yet additionally inspiring.

5. **Relational Elements:**

Character advancement in parody reaches out past individual development to envelop the complexities of relational elements. The connections characters structure with one another add to the comedic scene, setting out open doors for clever chitchat, comedic errors, and shared comedic encounters. The development of these connections turns into a focal component in making a comedic troupe that resounds with crowds.

The investigation of relational elements takes into consideration a different scope of comedic cooperations — whether it's the odd-couple matching, the comedic triplet, or the outfit cast with a horde of characters. These elements give a fruitful ground to creating humor, as characters play off one another's assets, shortcomings, and differentiating characteristics. The comedic science inside the gathering turns into a wellspring of both individual and aggregate humor.

6. **Flightiness and Disruption:**

Fruitful person advancement in satire frequently includes the component of capriciousness and disruption. Characters that make heads spin, challenge generalizations, and amaze crowds add to the by and large comedic newness of the account. Undermining laid out standards takes into account startling comedic exciting bends in the road, keeping the crowd connected with and pleased.

This flightiness can appear in different ways, from characters settling on startling decisions to testing customary comedic figures of speech. At the point when characters shock the crowd with activities or responses that veer off from the expected, it adds a layer of eccentricism that improves the comedic experience. Disruption turns into a method for opposing comedic shows, infusing inventiveness and curiosity into the story.

7. **Adjusting Consistency and Shock:**

A fragile equilibrium exists between keeping up with consistency in character qualities and presenting astounding components that keep the crowd captivated. Consistency guarantees that characters stay consistent with their laid out characters, giving a feeling of commonality and unwavering quality. Then again, shocks and unforeseen improvements keep characters from becoming unsurprising, injecting the story with a feeling of energy.

The test for narrators lies in exploring this equilibrium, permitting characters to develop and advance while saving the comedic quintessence that charmed them to crowds in any case. When executed actually, this equilibrium brings about characters that vibe genuine, dynamic, and fit for amazing crowds with comedic turns that resound inside the laid out account structure.

6.2 Exploring Dark Comedy

Investigating dull satire includes exploring the complicated territory where humor and uneasiness converge, making an exceptional space for narrating that challenges traditional standards. Dull satire, otherwise called dark parody, blossoms with tending to no subjects, awkward real factors, and the idiocies of life from a perspective of humor. This investigation dives into the subtleties of dim satire, looking at its qualities, request, and the sensitive equilibrium it strikes among giggling and distress.

1. **Embracing the Untouchable:**
   Dim satire flourishes with pushing the limits of cultural restrictions and tending to subjects that may be viewed as forbidden in regular humor. It digs into the awkward parts of human experience, investigating subjects like demise, disease, wrongdoing, and cultural issues with a comedic focal point. By embracing the untouchable, dull parody moves crowds to face the uneasiness related with these subjects and track down humor in the apparently improper.

   The investigation of no subjects in dim parody frequently fills a double need — evoking chuckling while likewise provoking reflection on cultural standards and values. This rebellious methodology permits dim comedies to give an exceptional critique on the human condition, involving humor as a focal point through which to view and scrutinize the awkward real factors of life.

2. **Incongruity and Parody:**

   At the center of dull parody lies incongruity and parody. The class frequently utilizes these abstract gadgets to evaluate and caricaturize cultural standards, organizations, and individual ways of behaving. By involving humor as a device for social editorial, dim comedies explore the scarce difference among entertainment and investigate, provoking crowds to scrutinize their presumptions and points of view.

   Sarcastic components in dim parody can appear in different ways, from taunting social shows to uncovering the ludicrousness of specific convictions or practices. The utilization of incongruity permits narrators to cause circumstances where the surprising and problematic become wellsprings of humor, featuring the innate inconsistencies inside human instinct and society.

3. **Hangman's tree Humor:**

   A central trait of dim parody is its use of hangman's tree humor — a type of humor that arises even with dismal or dangerous circumstances. This kind of humor permits characters and crowds to adapt to misfortune or distress by tracking down silliness and giggling amidst desperate conditions. It frequently fills in as a way of dealing with stress, giving a delivery valve to pressure and uneasiness.

   Scaffold humor can be tracked down in different settings, from the exchange among clinical experts managing provoking cases to characters exploring existential emergencies. By embracing hangman's tree humor, dim comedies change possibly troubling circumstances into comedic minutes, offering a special viewpoint on the human capacity to find chuckling even despite difficulty.

4. **Complex Characters and Ethical quality:**

   Dull comedies frequently highlight ethically uncertain or defective characters whose activities challenge traditional ideas of good and bad. These characters explore an ethically dim scene, and their sketchy choices become a wellspring of both inconvenience and humor. The intricacy of characters in dull comedies adds profundity to the story, as crowds are constrained to wrestle with the moral ramifications of their activities.

Investigating profound quality in dim satire includes introducing characters who resist customary ideas of valor or villainy. The line among good and bad becomes obscured, and crowds are stood up to with the awkward reality that even ethically equivocal activities can be wellsprings of humor. This intricacy adds layers to the narrating, welcoming crowds to participate in a more nuanced assessment of character inspirations and decisions.

5. **The Silly and Strange:**

Dull satire frequently consolidates components of the ridiculous and strange to uplift its comedic influence. By presenting circumstances or characters that make no sense and reason, dim comedies make an other reality where the startling turns into the standard.

The utilization of ludicrousness enhances the humor, moving crowds to suspend their mistrust and embrace the whimsical.

Strange components in dim satire can go from ludicrous unexpected developments to characters with misrepresented characteristics or ways of behaving. This takeoff from reality adds a layer of eccentricism, upgrading the generally speaking comedic experience. The combination of the dim and the strange permits narrators to create accounts that enamor crowds with their flightiness and challenge their view of the real world.

6. **Crowd Commitment and Therapy:**

Dull parody draws in crowds in a remarkable way by expecting them to wrestle with distress while likewise welcoming them to track down humor in eccentric spots. The chuckling evoked from dull satire is much of the time joined by a feeling of therapy — an arrival of repressed strain and disquiet. The class gives a space to crowds to stand up to awkward bits of insight, question cultural standards, and experience a type of profound delivery through giggling.

The commitment with dim satire requires a specific degree of liberality and a readiness to defy awkward topic. It provokes crowds to move past their usual ranges of familiarity, inciting them to reexamine their points of view and track down humor in the unforeseen. The soothing experience got from dull satire is a demonstration of its capacity to get certified close to home reactions while as yet conveying snapshots of giggling.

1. **The Fine Line between Dark and Offensive**

The scarcely discernible difference between dim satire and disagreeableness is a fragile and frequently discussed domain, where narrators explore the intricacies of humor that tracks on the edge of uneasiness. Dull parody, known for its investigation of no subjects and cultural evaluate through humor, can at times push limits that challenge ordinary standards. In any case, the qualification between dull parody that resounds and humor that becomes hostile is a nuanced thought that includes grasping setting, aim, and the effect on the crowd.

1. **Setting and Subtlety:**
   One of the vital elements in knowing the scarcely discernible difference between dim satire and obnoxiousness is the significance of setting and subtlety. Relevant comprehension includes thinking about the particular conditions, characters, and story components inside which the dim comedic components unfurl. The subtleties of narrating, character improvement, and the general account bend assume a urgent part in deciding if the humor lines up with the tone of the story or drifts into a hostile area.

   For instance, a very much created dim parody could utilize humor to caricaturize cultural issues or challenge restrictions inside a painstakingly built story system. Interestingly, hostile humor might miss the mark on profundity and subtlety important to contextualize its substance, depending exclusively on shock esteem without adding to the by and large narrating.

2. **Purpose and Sarcastic Analysis:**
The purpose behind dim satire is a huge figure separating it from hostile humor. Dim comedies frequently utilize parody to offer a basic discourse on cultural standards, establishments, or human way of behaving. The aim isn't only to incite for shock however to involve humor as an instrument for social investigate and thoughtfulness. At the point when the basic role is humorous and pointed toward featuring idiocies or addressing shows, dim parody keeps up with its creative and account respectability.

Then again, hostile humor might come up short on noticeable goal past incitement or the longing to stun. Without a reasonable reason or ironical component, hostile humor can estrange crowds and chance sustaining unsafe generalizations or building up regrettable cultural perspectives.

3. **Compassion and Awareness:**
Understanding the line between dim parody and unsavoriness requires a sharp familiarity with compassion and responsiveness. Dull comedies frequently prevail with regards to pushing limits since they approach awkward subjects with a comprehension of the human experience, utilizing compassion to interface with the crowd. This compassionate methodology takes into account the investigation of troublesome points without dismissing the profound effect they might have on people.

Hostile humor, then again, may need awareness and compassion, excusing the expected damage or close to home cost it might force on specific people or networks. The shortfall of thought for the sentiments and encounters of others can prompt the view of the substance as hostile instead of interesting.

4. **Influence on Minimized Gatherings:**
The effect on minimized bunches is a basic calculate assessing

whether humor falls inside the domain of dim parody or wanders into repulsiveness. Dim comedies that integrate components of parody frequently challenge cultural power structures and give a stage to underestimated voices. When done mindfully, this can add to social advancement and animate significant discussions. Then again, hostile humor might sustain hurtful generalizations, support oppressive perspectives, or minimize currently weak gatherings. The effect on the crowd, particularly the individuals who have a place with minimized networks, turns into a urgent part of deciding if the humor is crossing moral limits.

5. **Social Awareness:**

Social awareness is fundamental in knowing the almost negligible difference between dull parody and unpleasantness. Humor that objectives explicit societies, nationalities, or foundations without understanding or thought can undoubtedly become hostile. Dim comedies that consolidate social components ought to do as such with deference, staying away from propagation of destructive generalizations or the minimization of social encounters.

Social responsiveness includes perceiving the variety of points of view and encounters inside the crowd and recognizing the potential mischief that hostile humor can cause. Narrators should know about the effect their substance might have on various networks and endeavor to make accounts that cultivate inclusivity as opposed to propagating generalizations.

6. **Dependable Narrating:**

At last, the barely recognizable difference between dull satire and repulsiveness highlights the significance of dependable narrating. Narrators have an obligation to move toward their specialty with mindfulness, taking into account the likely results of their substance. This obligation includes a guarantee to mindfulness, compassion, and a comprehension of the social and social ramifications of the stories they build.

While dull parody can be an incredible asset for social critique, narrators should explore this landscape with care, guaranteeing that their aim is clear, their substance is logically fitting, and they stay delicate to the expected effect on their crowd. The scarcely discernible difference requests a cognizant work to offset creative articulation with moral contemplations, perceiving that humor can incite thought without turning to offense.

b. Using Taboo Topics for Humor

Involving no themes for humor includes a fragile equilibrium of mind, setting, and responsiveness, testing cultural standards while evoking giggling. No subjects, frequently viewed as untouchable in traditional talk, become rich ground for comedic investigation when drawn nearer nicely. This investigation digs into the subtleties of utilizing untouchable subjects in humor, analyzing how narrators explore the barely recognizable difference among incitement and comedic understanding.

1. **Mocking Social Editorial:**
   One of the essential ways untouchable points can be actually utilized for humor is through mocking social analysis. Dull comedies frequently influence humor to evaluate cultural standards, foundations, or social practices. By tending to restrictions inside the setting of parody, narrators can incite thought and brief crowds to address laid out convictions. This approach takes into consideration a more profound investigation of complicated issues while implanting the story with humor that fills a need past simple shock esteem.

2. **Testing Generalizations and Suppositions:**
   Humor got from no themes can act as a device for testing generalizations and suppositions. By uncovering the silliness or inconsistencies inside cultural assumptions, narrators can utilize parody to disturb imbued convictions. This approach welcomes crowds to rethink their predispositions and take part in a more

nuanced reflection on subjects that could somehow be kept away from in discussion. Testing generalizations through humor adds to the destroying of hurtful confusions and advances a more open exchange.

3. **Way of dealing with stress and Therapy:**

Involving no subjects in humor can likewise work as a way of dealing with stress and give a feeling of therapy. Parody, particularly dim or scaffold humor, permits people to defy awkward or troubling subjects in a manner that eases the close to home burden. At the point when introduced inside the setting of narrating, humor turns into a restorative device, offering crowds a delivery from pressure and a valuable chance to track down levity despite difficulty. This therapeutic capability permits untouchable points to be tended to with a level of profound responsiveness.

4. **Reflecting Human Idiocies:**

No points frequently address the idiocies innate in human encounters and ways of behaving. Parody got from these subjects can focus a light on the madness of specific cultural standards or individual activities, inciting reflection on the inborn inconsistencies inside human instinct. By outlining untouchable subjects inside the focal point of idiocy, narrators welcome crowds to snicker at the idiosyncrasies of the human condition while empowering a more basic assessment of winning standards.

5. **Relevant Contemplations:**

The viability of involving untouchable points for humor depends intensely on logical contemplations. The manner by which these subjects are incorporated into the account, the profundity of character improvement, and the general subjects of the story all add to the gathering of the humor. Setting turns into a significant figure guaranteeing that the utilization of no subjects lines up with the general tone and goal of the narrating, keeping the humor from seeming needless or hostile.

6. **Crowd Mindfulness and Responsiveness:**
   Exploring untouchable subjects in humor requires a sharp familiarity with the crowd and aversion to expected responses. Narrators should think about the assorted viewpoints inside their crowd and recognize the potential effect that specific subjects might have on people or networks. Laying out a harmony between testing cultural standards and keeping away from hurt is fundamental to making content that is interesting without being unnecessarily provocative.

7. **Moral Obligation:**

Narrators bear a moral obligation while involving untouchable subjects for humor. This obligation includes a promise to insightful narrating that thinks about the possible outcomes of the substance. Moral contemplations reach out to the effect on underestimated gatherings, social responsiveness, and a comprehension of the potential damage that hostile humor might cause. Maintaining moral guidelines guarantees that humor got from no subjects adds to significant discourse as opposed to sustaining hurtful generalizations or building up regrettable cultural mentalities.

Chapter 7

Crafting a Comedic Voice

Creating a comedic voice is a nuanced and mind boggling try that includes sharpening a remarkable style, viewpoint, and conveyance to evoke chuckling. Whether through composed content, stand-up exhibitions, or different mediums, the improvement of a comedic voice is an excursion that requires a profound comprehension of humor, mindfulness, and a sharp feeling of timing. This investigation dives into the diverse course of creating a comedic voice, looking at the key components that add to the peculiarity and viability of humor.

1. **Understanding Humor Styles:**

   At the core of creating a comedic voice is a significant comprehension of humor styles. Humor is different and emotional, incorporating different structures like parody, droll, pleasantry, observational satire, and the sky is the limit from there. Each style has its own arrangement of shows, rhythms, and requests. Fruitful joke artists frequently explore different avenues regarding various styles to find what resounds most legitimately with their voice. This understanding takes into consideration the deliberate choice and fuse of humor styles that line up with the joke artist's sensibilities and expected comedic influence.

2. **Embracing Credibility:**

Credibility is the foundation of a convincing comedic voice. Embracing one's certifiable self, encounters, and points of view frames the reason for a comedic persona that feels bona fide and interesting. Crowds associate with entertainers who share their actual selves, tracking down humor in the peculiarities, quirks, and weaknesses that make every individual novel. Making a comedic voice includes digging one's own life for comedic material, uncovering individual stories, and being unafraid to investigate the certified, some of the time muddled, parts of the human experience.

3. **Observational Abilities:**

A sharp feeling of perception is an indispensable part of making a comedic voice. Comics frequently draw motivation from their general surroundings, noticing ordinary circumstances, human way of behaving, and cultural standards with a silly focal point. By developing an elevated familiarity with the idiocies and subtleties in the common, entertainers can change unremarkable encounters into comedic gold. This observational expertise takes into consideration the production of material that reverberates with crowds on a common, engaging level.

4. **Fostering a One of a kind Point of view:**

Creating a comedic voice includes fostering a one of a kind point of view that separates the comic from others. This viewpoint includes how the comic perspectives the world, deciphers occasions, and explores through life's idiocies. Whether it's a pessimistic standpoint, a hopeful focal point, or an inclination for humility, a particular viewpoint turns into the mark stamp of a comedic voice. The development of this interesting perspective includes self-reflection, contemplation, and an eagerness to embrace one's uniqueness.

5. **Playing with Persona:**
   Joke artists frequently explore different avenues regarding persona, taking on misrepresented or adapted forms of themselves as a component of their comedic voice. This persona fills in as a comedic device, improving specific parts of the comic's character for hilarious impact. This can include enhancing idiosyncrasies, embracing character qualities, or in any event, making altogether fictitious personas. Playing with persona considers a powerful scope of comedic articulation, adding flexibility to the comic's voice and empowering them to investigate a range of comedic styles.

6. **Dominating Timing and Conveyance:**
   Timing and conveyance are key components of making a comedic voice. A very much planned zinger or an impeccably conveyed jest can hoist common material into comedic brightness. The specialty of comedic timing includes a natural comprehension of musicality, pacing, and the essential position of zingers. Entertainers frequently refine their conveyance through training, calibrating the subtleties of tone, rhythm, and stops to amplify the effect of their humor.

7. **Associating with the Crowd:**
   Making a comedic voice reaches out past individual articulation to laying out an association with the crowd. Effective jokesters are sensitive to the responses and criticism of their crowd, changing their conveyance in view of the energy in the room. The capacity to peruse the crowd's reaction, draw in with them, and make a common encounter adds to the reverberation of a comedic voice. This association encourages a climate where chuckling turns into a mutual and intuitive experience.

8. **Trial and error and Development:**
   The method involved with making a comedic voice is iterative and dynamic. Comics participate in ceaseless trial and error, refining their material in view of crowd responses and self-improvement.

The eagerness to develop and adjust is a sign of fruitful comedic voices. It implies facing imaginative challenges, investigating new comedic styles, and being available to the advancement of one's persona and material after some time.

9. **Tracking down Equilibrium:**

Creating a comedic voice requires tracking down a harmony among consistency and versatility. While keeping a center comedic character and style, jokesters likewise should be adaptable and receptive to evolving elements, tastes, and social movements. Finding some kind of harmony guarantees that the comedic voice stays valid, important, and strong despite developing comedic scenes.

10. **Embracing the Capricious:**

Satire flourishes with the unusual, and creating a comedic voice includes embracing the unforeseen. The capacity to explore unanticipated conditions, answer unconstrained collaborations with the crowd, and consolidate extemporization adds to the unique idea of a comedic voice. Embracing the flighty adds a component of shock, keeping exhibitions new and locking in.

11. **Nonstop Refinement:**

Making a comedic voice is an excursion of persistent refinement. Joke artists sharpen their art through determined work on, composing, and refining material. This interaction includes self-investigate, looking for input from companions and tutors, and a promise to consistent improvement. The commitment to refining comedic abilities guarantees that the voice stays dynamic, resounding, and fit for adjusting to assorted crowds and settings.

7.1 Developing a Unique Style

Fostering an extraordinary style is a groundbreaking excursion for any craftsman, and in the domain of parody, it turns into a particular mark that separates one from the group. A humorist's style incorporates a blend of conveyance, persona, material, and, surprisingly, the mood of their exhibition.

This investigation digs into the complicated course of fostering an interesting comedic style, revealing insight into the fundamental components that add to the formation of a comedic persona that reverberates really with crowds.

1. **Self-Investigation and Validness:**
   At the center of fostering an extraordinary comedic style is the excursion of self-investigation and embracing credibility. Entertainers leave on a course of contemplation to figure out their own encounters, viewpoints, and mannerisms. By diving into individual accounts, eccentricities, and weaknesses, comics find the unrefined substance that shapes the underpinning of their remarkable comedic voice. Validness turns into the standard for making a style that feels certified and engaging to crowds.

2. **Mining Individual Encounters:**
   The extravagance of a jokester's material frequently lies in digging individual encounters for comedic gold. Whether it's describing humiliating minutes, analyzing familial elements, or considering life's idiocies, individual encounters act as a wellspring of engaging and clever substance. Fostering a novel style includes the cunning curation of these encounters, changing them into stories, zingers, and perceptions that mirror the comic's particular point of view.

3. **Embracing Weakness:**
   Weakness is a powerful fixing in the speculative chemistry of fostering an exceptional comedic style. Entertainers who will uncover their weaknesses, share close stories, and giggle at their own blemishes make an association with crowds. Embracing weakness considers a more profound degree of commitment, as crowds perceive the realness in the comic's presentation. This transparency turns into a characterizing element of the comedic style, charming the comic to crowds who appreciate the certifiable and unfiltered depiction of the human experience.

4. **Trial and error with Persona:**
   Creating a special comedic style frequently includes trial and error with persona. Comics might embrace overstated forms of themselves, investigate imaginary people, or play with parts of their character to intensify comedic impact. Persona turns into a powerful instrument for upgrading specific qualities, eccentricities, or attributes that add to the in general comedic character. This trial and error considers flexibility in execution and the production of a paramount and unmistakable comedic persona.

5. **Observational Bits of knowledge:**
   A sharp feeling of perception is a major part of fostering an extraordinary comedic style. Entertainers improve their observational abilities, definitely noticing their general surroundings to reveal the idiocies, subtleties, and characteristics of regular daily existence. From cultural patterns to individual ways of behaving, these experiences become grain for creating material that reverberates with crowds. The capacity to distil sharp perceptions into amusing editorial adds layers to the comedic style, giving profundity and significance.

6. **Integrating Impacts Nicely:**
   While each comic tries to foster a style that is exceptionally their own, it's unavoidable that they will be impacted by the comedic voices that preceded them. The vital lies in consolidating these impacts mindfully. Instead of emulating or repeating, fruitful joke artists absorb assorted impacts, adjusting them to suit their own voice. This union of impacts adds to the development of a style that is a veritable impression of the comic's independence.

7. **Calibrating Conveyance and Timing:**
   The dominance of conveyance and timing is a fine art inside comedic style advancement. Jokesters calibrate their conveyance, exploring different avenues regarding different tones, pacing, and expressions to amplify the effect of their material. A very much planned zinger, a flawlessly executed stop, or a decisively changed

tone can change normal substance into comedic brightness. The development of an extraordinary style includes a careful sharpening of these conveyance and timing subtleties.

8. **Creating a Conspicuous Presence:**

   An exceptional comedic style reaches out past the jokes and material to incorporate a conspicuous presence. This presence incorporates perspectives like non-verbal communication, stage disposition, and, surprisingly, the joke artist's design decisions. The making of a conspicuous presence improves the general effect of the comedic style, engraving an enduring picture in the personalities of crowds. It turns into a visual and experiential part that supplements the verbal and comedic components of the exhibition.

9. **Adjusting to Various Crowds:**

   Flexibility is a sign of an advanced comedic style. Entertainers proficient at adjusting their material to various crowds show a dominance of their specialty. While keeping up with the center components of their style, humorists might change their methodology, language, or social references to resound with different groups. This flexibility guarantees that the comedic style stays dynamic and available across different execution settings.

10. **Developing Consistency:**

    While flexibility is significant, developing consistency inside the comedic style is similarly significant. Consistency includes keeping a conspicuous string that goes through exhibitions, making a firm personality that crowds can interface with. Whether through repeating subjects, repeating characters, or a steady comedic viewpoint, developing a feeling of consistency adds to the foundation of a comedic brand.

11. **Crowd Commitment:**

    The improvement of a novel comedic style is a cooperative interaction that includes crowd commitment. Jokesters check crowd responses, change their conveyance in light of criticism, and construct a compatibility that improves the generally speaking comedic experience.

The capacity to interface with crowds on an individual level, to peruse their energy, and to draw in them in the comedic venture is a vital part of fostering an unmistakable style.

12. **Nonstop Development:**

The excursion of fostering a special comedic style is a continuous course of development. Comics embrace the requirement for nonstop development, refinement, and variation. As entertainers gain insight, experience new impacts, and explore shifts in their own lives, their comedic style advances naturally. This constant development guarantees that the comedic style stays applicable, new, and lined up with the comic's developing voice.

1. **Finding Your Comic Persona**

Finding your comic persona is an extraordinary excursion that includes self-disclosure, trial and error, and a profound comprehension of your comedic voice. A comic persona is something beyond a phase character; a refined rendition of yourself interfaces really with a crowd of people. This investigation digs into the unpredictable course of finding and developing your comic persona, revealing insight into the fundamental components that add to the improvement of a comedic character that reverberates with realness and humor.

1. **Self-Reflection and Genuineness:**
The underpinning of finding your comic persona lies in self-reflection and embracing credibility. Carve out opportunity to investigate your own encounters, viewpoints, and characteristics. Ponder what compels you giggle, your interesting perspective, and the parts of your character that stick out. Credibility is the

way to fashioning a veritable association with your crowd, as they answer the genuineness and appeal of your comedic persona.

2. **Distortion and Enhancement:**
One of the methodologies in finding your comic persona includes embellishment and enhancement of specific characteristics or idiosyncrasies. Recognize parts of your character, propensities, or responses that have comedic potential. By enhancing these qualities, you make an awesome rendition of yourself that turns into the comedic point of convergence. This distortion fills in as a comedic gadget, adding profundity and uniqueness to your comic persona.

3. **Distinguishing Extraordinary Characteristics:**
Each individual has novel characteristics or quirks that can act as comedic gold. These characteristics can go from unconventional propensities to unmistakable actual peculiarities. Distinguish the eccentricities that hang out in your daily existence, as they give significant material to making a noteworthy comic persona. Embrace these peculiarities as a feature of your comedic character, transforming them into comedic resources that put you aside.

4. **Observational Satire:**
Observational satire assumes a critical part in molding your comic persona. Develop a sharp feeling of perception and apply it to your general surroundings. What idiocies or idiosyncrasies do you see in regular day to day existence? Observational experiences become a wellspring of engaging material that can be coordinated into your comic persona. By sharing your exceptional viewpoints on common circumstances, you welcome crowds to see the world through your comedic focal point.

5. **Trial and error with Conveyance Styles:**
Finding your comic persona includes exploring different avenues regarding different conveyance styles. Evaluate different tones, pacing, and rhythms to see what reverberates best with your comedic voice. Consider how you need to introduce yourself in

front of an audience - whether it's through lifeless conveyance, high energy tricks, or a laid-back disposition. The trial and error with conveyance styles permits you to find the subtleties that improve the viability of your comedic persona.

6. **Adjusting Weakness and Certainty:**

An effective comic persona finds some kind of harmony among weakness and certainty. While weakness permits crowds to associate with your mankind, certainty guarantees that your comedic conveyance is significant. Embrace weakness by sharing individual stories, uncovering humiliating minutes, or talking about engaging battles. At the same time, ooze trust in your stage presence and conveyance to order the crowd's consideration.

7. **Integrating Individual Stories:**

Individual stories are strong instruments for fostering a comic persona. Share tales from your life, injected with humor and mindfulness. These individual stories give realness to your comedic persona as well as permit crowds to connect with your encounters. By meshing individual stories into your material, you make a rich embroidery that characterizes your comic personality.

8. **Embracing Uniqueness:**

Your uniqueness is your most noteworthy resource in tracking down your comic persona. Embrace the angles that make you stick out, regardless of whether they go amiss from ordinary comedic standards. Whether it's your unpredictable perspective, particular awareness of what's actually funny, or capricious conveyance style, inclining toward your uniqueness cultivates a unique and essential comic persona.

9. **Looking for Crowd Criticism:**

Crowd criticism is important during the time spent sharpening your comic persona. Focus on crowd responses - what jokes land well, when chuckling is most powerful, and how the crowd answers various parts of your conveyance. This criticism circle permits you to refine and change your comic persona in view of ongoing crowd responses, guaranteeing that your comedic character reverberates really.

10. **Adjusting to Various Crowds:**

While your comic persona is an unmistakable piece of your character, it ought to likewise be versatile to various crowds. An adaptable comic persona permits you to interface with different groups, changing your material or conveyance to suit shifted inclinations. The capacity to adjust guarantees that your comedic persona stays dynamic and available in various execution settings.

11. **Consistency in Marking:**

Consistency in marking adds to the acknowledgment and memorability of your comic persona. Consider how you need to be seen by crowds - your stage name, style of dress, and, surprisingly, the manner in which you collaborate with the crowd. Keeping a reliable brand builds up the character of your comic persona, making an unmistakable presence that waits in the personalities of crowds.

12. **Persistent Advancement:**

Finding your comic persona is certainly not a static cycle however a constant development. As you gain insight, experience new impacts, and explore shifts in your own life, your comedic persona develops naturally. Be available to development, refinement, and variation. Embrace the excursion of constant development, guaranteeing that your comic persona stays important, new, and lined up with your developing comedic voice.

b. Experimenting with Different Comic Styles

Exploring different avenues regarding different comic styles is a dynamic and groundbreaking excursion that permits jokesters to investigate different roads of humor, refine their specialty, and find the comedic voice that reverberates most truly with both themselves and their crowd. This investigation includes the deliberate investigation of different comedic styles, each with its one of a kind shows, tones, and requests. Comics take part in trial and error to recognize the styles that line up with their sensibilities and grandstand their comedic ability.

1. **Parody and Social Discourse:**
   One of the comic styles that entertainers frequently investigate is parody, a type of humor that utilizes incongruity, misrepresentation, or criticism to scrutinize and deride cultural issues, foundations, or people. Mocking satire permits comics to dive into social and political discourse, offering an entertaining focal point through which crowds can consider the idiocies of the world. This style requires a sharp mind, sharp perception, and the capacity to distil complex issues into gnawing, entertaining critique.

2. **Droll and Actual Parody:**
   Droll parody, portrayed by overstated actual activities, ridiculous circumstances, and visual gags, is one more style that comics explore different avenues regarding.
   This type of parody depends on the rawness of the entertainer, underscoring visual humor and misrepresented responses. Entertainers might take part in flummoxes, sight gags, or droll schedules to evoke giggling. Dominating droll requires immaculate timing and a sharp comprehension of actual satire's immortal allure.

3. **Stand-Up Parody:**
   Stand-up satire is a flexible and generally rehearsed style that puts the comic alone in front of an audience, drawing in the crowd through a discourse loaded up with jokes, tales, and observational humor. Entertainers explore different avenues regarding rise up to refine their conveyance, timing, and the craft of interfacing with a group of people. Stand-up considers individual narrating, observational experiences, and direct commitment with the group, making it a basic style that numerous comics investigate and dominate.

4. **Improvisational Satire:**
   Improvisational or comedy satire includes unscripted exhibitions

where jokesters cause situations, characters, and discourse on the spot. This style sharpens fast reasoning, flexibility, and co-operative abilities as jokesters respond to startling prompts or circumstances. Trying different things with comedy encourages suddenness, imagination, and the capacity to think and react quickly, adding to a jokester's by and large comedic tool stash.

5. **Dull Parody and Scaffold Humor:**

   Dull parody investigates no or bleak subjects with humor, frequently tending to delicate points like demise, sickness, or misfortune. Humorists exploring different avenues regarding dim parody explore the scarcely discernible difference among giggling and uneasiness, utilizing mind to reveal insight into the hazier parts of life. This style requires a cautious harmony between responsiveness and boldness, moving crowds to track down humor in the most hopeless of conditions.

6. **Character Satire:**

   Character parody includes joke artists embracing explicit personas or making fictitious people to convey their humor. These characters might have unmistakable voices, actual qualities, or character attributes that upgrade comedic impact. Exploring different avenues regarding character parody permits entertainers to exhibit flexibility, showiness, and the capacity to occupy assorted jobs, carrying a dramatic aspect to their exhibitions.

7. **Strange and Absurdist Parody:**

   Strange and absurdist parody investigates the peculiar, irrational, and fantastical, making humor from the disjointed qualities of the creative mind. Entertainers explore different avenues regarding oddity by creating situations, characters, or stories that challenge regular rationale. This style requests an eagerness to embrace the outlandish and challenge the limits of the real world, welcoming crowds into an existence where the surprising rules.

8. **Wit and Quip Based Satire:**

   Wit and quips are comedic styles that middle on phonetic

keenness and risqué statement. Humorists explore different avenues regarding clever pleasantry, creating jokes that depend on the subtleties of language, homophones, and astute turns. This style requires a sharp comprehension of language, a talent for shrewd pleasantry, and the capacity to convey plays on words with flawless timing.

9. **Narrating Parody:**

Narrating parody includes winding around drawing in accounts loaded up with humor, tales, and engaging encounters. Jokesters exploring different avenues regarding narrating improve their skill to enthrall crowds through convincing stories. This style frequently considers further associations with the crowd as entertainers share individual stories, making a common encounter that resounds on an engaging level.

10. **Melodic Parody:**

Melodic satire consolidates humor with melodic components, integrating tunes, spoofs, or comedic verses into exhibitions. Comics explore different avenues regarding melodic satire to grandstand their flexibility, coordinating melodic ability into their comedic collection. This style might include playing instruments, singing clever tunes, or making melodic dramas that add a melodic aspect to the parody.

11. **Mockumentary and Character Broiling:**

Mockumentary-style parody includes introducing fictitious occasions or characters in a narrative configuration, frequently obscuring the lines among the real world and fiction. Character simmering, then again, is a comedic style where humorists mock or ridicule explicit people, genuine or fanciful. The two styles require a nuanced comprehension of character elements, viable narrating, and the capacity to extricate humor from the eccentricities and imperfections of people.

12. **Meta Satire and Breaking the Fourth Wall:**

Meta parody includes mindful humor that recognizes the shows of satire itself. Comics exploring different avenues regarding meta satire might break the fourth wall, tending to the crowd straightforwardly, or energetically dismantling comedic figures of speech. This style requests a degree of mindfulness, mind, and a readiness to challenge conventional comedic limits.

7.2 Navigating Cultural Sensitivities

Exploring social responsive qualities in satire is a sensitive and complex undertaking that expects entertainers to adjust the quest for humor with deference for different points of view and characters.

Satire has the ability to unite individuals, however it likewise conveys the obligation of thinking about the effect of jokes on different social gatherings. This investigation dives into the subtleties of exploring social awarenesses in satire, analyzing the difficulties, moral contemplations, and procedures for cultivating inclusivity and understanding.

1. **Social Mindfulness and Exploration:**

   The establishment for exploring social responsive qualities starts with social mindfulness and intensive examination. Joke artists should focus on figuring out the accounts, customs, and awarenesses of various social gatherings. This information gives the setting important to make humor that is educated, aware, and aware of possible responsive qualities. Research permits jokesters to abstain from sustaining generalizations or coincidentally irritating crowds in view of social misconceptions.

2. **Figuring out Generalizations and Staying away from Hurtful Sayings:**

   Comics should be careful about keeping away from destructive generalizations and sayings that propagate negative presumptions about social or ethnic gatherings. While humor frequently includes misrepresentation and speculation, depending on destructive generalizations can build up predispositions and add to a culture of bias. Figuring out the effect of specific sayings and effectively keeping away from them is critical for mindful and socially delicate parody.

3. **Punching Up versus Punching Down:**

A critical thought in exploring social responsive qualities is the rule of "punching up" versus "punching down." Punching up includes focusing on those in, influential places, authority, or honor, involving humor as a device for social study. Conversely, punching down includes making jokes to the detriment of minimized or weak gatherings. Humorists focused on social awareness endeavor to punch up, utilizing their satire to challenge cultural standards and power structures as opposed to sustaining hurt.

4. **Multifacetedness and Layered Personalities:**

Perceiving the diversity of people's personalities is fundamental in exploring social awarenesses. Individuals have a place with different social, ethnic, or gatherings at the same time, and their encounters are molded by the crossing point of these characters. Comics should be sensitive to the subtleties of interconnection, staying away from distorted depictions that disregard the intricacies of people's layered characters.

5. **The Force of Humility:**

Jokesters frequently influence humble humor as a device to interface with crowds. While investigating social subjects, humility permits joke artists to explore awarenesses by turning the concentrate internal. By making fun of their own social foundation or encounters, humorists can encourage a feeling of inclusivity and shared giggling without focusing on others in a possibly hostile way.

6. **Cooperative Satire and Various Voices:**

Consolidating different voices and viewpoints in the parody business is critical for exploring social responsive qualities successfully. Cooperative satire endeavors that include people from various social foundations bring a lavishness of encounters and bits of knowledge to the innovative flow. Various voices add to a more nuanced, comprehensive, and socially delicate comedic scene.

7. **Criticism and Open Exchange:**

Laying out an open discourse with crowds and being responsive to input is an essential piece of exploring social awarenesses. Entertainers ought to make spaces for crowd individuals to communicate their points of view, and they ought to ponder and gain from productive analysis. This input circle empowers comics to develop, refine their material, and guarantee that their satire remains socially delicate and applicable.

8. **Setting and Subtlety:**

Understanding the significance of setting and subtlety is fundamental in social responsiveness. A joke that may be generally welcomed in one setting could be improper or hostile in another. Joke artists need to consider the social setting where they are performing and designer their material in like manner. Subtlety considers a more exact and insightful way to deal with addressing social subjects without turning to expansive speculations.

9. **Aim versus Effect:**

Jokesters wrestle with the harmony among aim and effect while exploring social awarenesses. While the goal behind a joke might be harmless, the effect on the crowd can shift in light of their own encounters and points of view. Humorists should be sensitive to the expected effect of their material and reconsider and change in view of how their parody is gotten.

10. **Timing and Awareness:**

Timing assumes a vital part in exploring social responsive qualities. Entertainers ought to be aware of recent developments, cultural moves, and advancing sensibilities. What could have been OK or hilarious in the past may presently not be suitable, and humorists need to adjust their material to line up with the advancing social scene.

11. **Offering Options in contrast to Culpable Material:**
    Entertainers focused on social responsiveness can offer options in contrast to possibly affronting material. Rather than depending on generalizations or possibly hurtful jokes, humorists can investigate elective comedic points that challenge standards, question suppositions, or give new viewpoints without falling back on uncaring substance.

12. **Certified Statement of regret and Learning:**

In situations where an entertainer's material unexpectedly crosses social limits and causes hurt, a certified statement of regret is vital. Gaining from the experience, recognizing the effect of the coldhearted substance, and showing a pledge to development and training are fundamental stages in reconstructing entrust with crowds and networks impacted.

1. Avoiding Stereotypes

Staying away from generalizations in satire is a urgent part of making humor that is conscious, comprehensive, and free from propagating hurtful predispositions. Generalizations are distorted, frequently pessimistic, and summed up suspicions about specific gatherings in light of their race, nationality, orientation, religion, or different attributes. Comics assume a critical part in molding cultural points of view, and by avoiding generalizations, they add to a more smart and socially mindful comedic scene. This investigation digs into the significance of keeping away from generalizations in satire, the difficulties in question, and techniques for making humor that is both engaging and conscious.

1. **Grasping the Effect of Generalizations:**
   Entertainers should perceive and figure out the significant effect of generalizations on people and networks. Generalizations propagate destructive accounts, support predispositions, and add

to the minimization of specific gatherings. By recognizing the potential mischief brought about by generalizations, jokesters can pursue informed decisions to abstain from propagating these harming sayings in their comedic material.

2. **Testing Suspicions and Standards:**

One of the jobs of satire is to challenge cultural standards and question suspicions. Humorists can use their foundation to undermine generalizations by introducing elective viewpoints, testing assumptions, and featuring the idiocy of depending on expansive speculations. Parody turns into a useful asset for cultural scrutinize when it challenges as opposed to builds up generalizations.

3. **Punching Up As opposed to Punching Down:**

Jokesters can explore the aversion of generalizations by taking on the guideline of "punching up" rather than "punching down." Punching up includes coordinating humor toward those in, influential places, honor, or authority. By zeroing in on cultural designs as opposed to focusing on minimized or weak gatherings, entertainers can utilize their foundation to scrutinize power lopsided characteristics without sustaining destructive generalizations.

4. **Making Nuanced and Genuine Characters:**

While making characters for comedic representations or exhibitions, entertainers ought to take a stab at subtlety and credibility. Staying away from one-layered, cliché depictions requires digging into the intricacy of characters, giving them as people exceptional qualities, inspirations, and viewpoints. Bona fide characters reverberate all the more profoundly with crowds and try not to propagate unsafe generalizations.

5. **Various Portrayal in Parody:**

Guaranteeing assorted portrayal in parody is instrumental in staying away from generalizations. Joke artists from various foundations bring remarkable viewpoints, encounters, and social bits of knowledge to the comedic scene. At the point when different voices are incorporated, parody turns into a rich embroidery that difficulties generalizations and gives a more exact impression of the complex human experience.

6. **Parody and Satire with Care:**
   While parody and spoof can be powerful comedic devices, they require cautious execution to try not to support generalizations. While ridiculing or mocking explicit people or gatherings, joke artists ought to guarantee that the humor is established in analysis on cultural issues as opposed to propagating unsafe suppositions. Parody turns into an important device for social evaluate when it challenges generalizations as opposed to depending on them for chuckles.

7. **Welcoming Joint effort and Criticism:**
   Joke artists can effectively stay away from generalizations by welcoming joint effort and looking for input from people with different viewpoints. Making an open exchange guarantees that comedic material is checked by various voices, diminishing the probability of unintentionally propagating generalizations. Joint effort cultivates a climate where jokesters can learn, develop, and refine their material to line up with a more comprehensive and conscious comedic ethos.

8. **Developing Material with Awareness:**
   The comedic scene is dynamic, and cultural standards and sensibilities develop over the long haul. Jokesters should stay delicate to these movements and adjust their material appropriately. What might have been adequate in the past may now be viewed as obsolete or hostile. A guarantee to developing material with responsiveness exhibits a devotion to making parody that lines up with contemporary moral guidelines.

9. **Zeroing in on Individual Way of behaving:**
   At the point when humor includes discourse on social or social issues, it is fundamental for center around individual way

of behaving instead of making wide speculations about whole gatherings. By investigating explicit activities or mentalities, joke artists try not to propagate destructive generalizations that misrepresent the intricacies of different networks.

10. **Self-Reflection and Mindfulness:**

Joke artists ought to take part in customary self-reflection and develop mindfulness to evaluate their own predispositions and suspicions. This thoughtfulness permits comics to distinguish possible vulnerable sides and difficulties intrinsic in their material. A guarantee to progressing mindfulness adds to the formation of parody that is smart, deferential, and liberated from dependence on generalizations.

11. **Setting Matters:**

Understanding the significance of setting is fundamental in keeping away from generalizations. A joke or comedic premise that might be satisfactory in one setting could be improper or hostile in another. Jokesters ought to be receptive to the social, social, and verifiable setting in which they are performing to guarantee that their material is given awareness and subtlety.

12. **Responsiveness to Input:**

Comics should be receptive to input from crowds, companions, and networks impacted by their material. On the off chance that a joke is recognized as sustaining generalizations or inflicting damage, an eagerness to tune in, learn, and change is significant. Responsiveness to criticism shows a pledge to moral satire and a devotion to keeping away from hurt.

b. Respecting Diverse Perspectives

Regarding different viewpoints in parody is a principal part of making a comprehensive and socially touchy comedic scene. Satire, as a type of imaginative articulation, has the ability to unite individuals, challenge cultural standards, and give a stage to different voices to be heard. This investigation digs into the significance of regarding assorted points of view in parody, the difficulties in question, and techniques for encouraging a climate where various voices are recognized, esteemed, and celebrated.

1. **Embracing the Intricacy of Human Experience:**
   Regarding different viewpoints in parody starts with an affirmation of the extravagance and intricacy of the human experience. Individuals come from shifted foundations, societies, and different backgrounds, each bringing a special focal point through which they see the world. Satire can possibly mirror this variety, permitting crowds to track down humor in the common and particular parts of their encounters.

2. **Keeping away from Homogenization and Generalizations:**
   Homogenization and generalizations can upset the deferential portrayal of assorted points of view in satire. Jokesters should avoid diminishing people or whole gatherings to shortsighted, one-layered depictions. By trying not to generalizations and embrace the intricacy of different characters, satire turns into a space where realness and subtlety win.

3. **Enhancing Underrepresented Voices:**
   Regarding different viewpoints includes effectively enhancing underrepresented voices in the satire scene. Jokesters from minimized or underrepresented networks might confront extra difficulties in acquiring perceivability, and setting out open doors that grandstand their remarkable viewpoints is fundamental. Stages that purposefully raise different voices add to a more comprehensive and energetic comedic local area.

4. **Investigating Social Subtleties with Responsiveness:**
   While integrating social components into comedic material, aversion to social subtleties is central. Entertainers ought to move toward social references with deference, staying away from apportionment and guaranteeing that the humor is established in a comprehension of the social setting. By investigating social

subtleties with responsiveness, satire turns into a scaffold that encourages seeing instead of propagating false impressions.

5. **Recognizing Interconnection:**

Interconnection perceives that people hold numerous crossing characters, and these personalities impact their encounters. Regarding assorted viewpoints in parody includes recognizing diversity and understanding that people might explore the world through the crossing points of race, orientation, sexuality, and that's just the beginning. Parody that perceives and celebrates multifacetedness encourages a more complete and comprehensive portrayal of different points of view.

6. **Encouraging Comprehensive Composing Rooms:**

Comprehensive composing rooms assume an essential part in forming the comedic story. Regarding different points of view requires the purposeful consideration of scholars from various foundations, guaranteeing that different encounters and perspectives add to the production of comedic content. A different composing group carries extravagance to the material and mirrors a promise to addressing a wide range of points of view.

7. **Testing Inclinations and Presumptions:**

Satire has the ability to challenge predispositions and suspicions that might sustain hurtful generalizations. Humorists ought to utilize their foundation to address cultural standards, dismantle suppositions, and challenge inclinations. By introducing elective points of view and welcoming crowds to rethink assumptions, parody turns into an impetus for positive cultural change.

8. **Making Comprehensive Satire Spaces:**

Regarding different viewpoints includes making satire spaces that are comprehensive and inviting to crowds from varying backgrounds. Comics and settings ought to endeavor to develop a climate where individuals feel addressed, comprehended, and regarded. Comprehensive satire spaces urge a more extensive crowd to draw in with and appreciate comedic content.

9. **Exploring Restrictions with Care:**
   While satire frequently pushes limits, exploring restrictions requires cautious thought. Jokesters ought to move toward delicate points with sympathy, perceiving the expected effect of their material on various crowds. Regarding assorted points of view includes proceeding cautiously on subjects that might be setting off or hostile, guaranteeing that the quest for humor doesn't come to the detriment of underestimated networks.

10. **Observing Contrasts without Othering:**
    Regarding assorted points of view implies praising contrasts without sustaining an "othering" attitude. Parody ought to welcome crowds to see the value in the novel characteristics of different points of view without building up an order of significant worth. By encouraging a climate that celebrates variety without making divisions, satire turns into a binding together power.

11. **Recognizing Verifiable Setting:**
    Satire frequently meets with authentic accounts, and recognizing verifiable setting is critical in regarding assorted viewpoints. Humorists ought to know about the authentic ramifications of their material, particularly while managing points that have well established social or cultural importance. Aversion to verifiable setting guarantees that satire is given a familiarity with the enduring effect it can have.

12. **Continuous Instruction and Development:**

Comics focused on regarding assorted viewpoints take part in continuous schooling and self-improvement. Remaining informed about developing cultural standards, social moves, and arising points of view adds to a humorist's capacity to make material that is significant, conscious, and circumspect of different perspectives. The obligation to progressing schooling exhibits a commitment to mindful and comprehensive satire.

8

Chapter 8

Challenges and Triumphs

Exploring the universe of satire is an excursion set apart by a horde of difficulties and wins, a rollercoaster ride through the scenes of giggling, innovativeness, and flexibility. Jokesters face extraordinary obstacles as they endeavor to interface with crowds, challenge cultural standards, and explore the steadily developing scene of humor. This investigation digs into the difficulties and wins that portray the comedic venture, revealing insight into the ups and downs that shape the existences of those devoted to the specialty of making individuals chuckle.

1. **The Test of Subjectivity:**
   One of the inborn difficulties in parody lies in its subjectivity. What one individual finds amusing, another probably won't reverberate with by any stretch of the imagination. Joke artists explore the sensitive equilibrium of creating material that is generally appealing while at the same time recognizing the inborn variety in crowd inclinations. This subjectivity requires flexibility and an eagerness to acknowledge that only one out of every odd joke will land with each crowd.

2. **Win in Associating with Crowds:**
Regardless of the subjectivity of humor, one of the victories in parody is the otherworldly association manufactured with crowds. The capacity to make individuals from various foundations, societies, and encounters chuckle is a demonstration of the force of parody. At the point when a humorist effectively resounds with a crowd of people, making a common snapshot of delight, it denotes a victory that energizes their enthusiasm for the specialty.

3. **Exploring Restrictions and Limits:**
Joke artists frequently track on the edges of cultural restrictions and limits, testing standards and stretching the boundaries of worthiness. The test lies in exploring this territory with care, perceiving that humor can be a useful asset for social evaluate yet should be employed capably. Win comes through separating hindrances, testing biases, and utilizing humor to start discussions about delicate themes.

4. **Win Conquering Naysayers:**
Naysayers represent an exceptional test for humorists, disturbing the painstakingly created progression of a presentation. Win in satire is in many cases tracked down in the capable treatment of naysayers, transforming possible aggravations into open doors for unconstrained mind and crowd commitment. Comics who become amazing at managing harassers show their comedic ability as well as their capacity to keep up with control and order the stage.

5. **Adjusting Imagination and Business Achievement:**
The test of offsetting imaginative inventiveness with business achievement is a typical problem for comics. Exploring the assumptions for both imaginative honesty and monetary suitability can interest. Win is tracked down in the fragile dance of making content that resounds really with the entertainer's voice while

likewise engaging a more extensive crowd, finding some kind of harmony among masterfulness and business reasonability.

6. **Win of Self-Articulation:**

For some jokesters, win is tracked down in the proud articulation of their real selves. Parody turns into a vehicle for self-revelation and a stage to share individual stories, viewpoints, and experiences. Win is acknowledged when jokesters bravely embrace their uniqueness, permitting crowds to associate with the crude, unfiltered substance of the entertainer.

7. **The Test of Taking care of Analysis:**

Analysis is an unavoidable piece of the comedic venture, and the test lies in exploring criticism productively. Entertainers face the gamble of being misconstrued or, now and again, confronting unforgiving studies. Win is tracked down in the strength to gain from analysis, refine material, and develop as an entertainer without compromising imaginative vision.

8. **Win in Building a Fanbase:**

Building a dependable fanbase is a huge victory for humorists. In a swarmed and serious industry, the capacity to develop a devoted following addresses a jokester's mystique, appeal, and comedic expertise. Win is acknowledged when crowds snicker at the jokes as well as interface with the character and exceptional voice of the comic.

9. **The Test of Keeping up with Significance:**

Satire is steadily developing, and comics face the test of remaining important in a quickly changing social scene. Exploring the moving sands of cultural standards, patterns, and humor inclinations requires versatility and a sharp consciousness of the overall outlook. Win is tracked down in the capacity to advance with the times, staying new and full.

10. **Win in Conveying Effective Social Analysis:**

Numerous joke artists try to accomplish something other than engage; they plan to convey significant social discourse through their humor. Win in parody is frequently entwined with the capacity to utilize mind and parody to reveal insight into cultural issues, challenge treachery, and incite decisive idea. At the point when parody rises above simple chuckling and turns into a vehicle for social change, it denotes a significant victory.

11. **The Test of Innovation:**

    In a world immersed with content, the test of keeping up with creativity is a consistent battle for comics. The apprehension about falling into adages or reusing tired material poses a potential threat. Win is tracked down chasing new viewpoints, inventive methodologies, and a pledge to conveying content that feels valid and unmistakable.

12. **Win Defeating Anxiety in front of large audiences:**

    Anxiety in front of large audiences is quite difficult for humorists, especially those beginning their excursion. The victory over anxiety in front of large audiences, the capacity to step onto the stage with certainty, and order the consideration of a crowd of people are stupendous triumphs. Defeating the underlying nerves is a transitional experience that signals development and strength notwithstanding an overwhelming test.

13. **The Test of Tracking down Valuable open doors:**

    Breaking into the parody business and tracking down chances to perform can be a considerable test. The serious idea of the field and the battle to get gigs can dampen. Win is found in the constancy to persevere, search out open doors, and make one's way, even despite starting mishaps.

14. **Win of Diverse Allure:**

    In an undeniably globalized world, joke artists face the test of engaging crowds with assorted social foundations.

    Win is acknowledged when comics span social holes, conveying humor that rises above borders and resounds with individuals from different backgrounds. The capacity to figure out some shared interest in giggling turns into an amazing asset for encouraging social comprehension.

15. **The Test of Emotional wellness:**

The comedic venture frequently negatively affects emotional wellness, with the tensions of execution, the consistent journey for approval, and the weakness of showcasing oneself. Win in satire isn't just about chuckles yet in addition about keeping up with mental prosperity, looking for help when required, and finding an equilibrium that considers an economical and satisfying profession.

16. **Win in Heritage and Effect:**

For entertainers, a definitive victory lies in the enduring heritage they abandon. At the point when their humor rises above ages, shapes social discussions, and makes a permanent imprint on the comedic scene, they accomplish a type of everlasting status. Significant commitments to the work of art become a demonstration of a jokester's persevering through win.

In the erratic universe of parody, difficulties and wins are entwined, making a story that is as different and nuanced as the actual jokesters. Each zinger conveyed, each association fashioned with a crowd of people, and the versatility to explore the ups and downs add to the rich embroidered artwork of the comedic venture. The difficulties become venturing stones, and the victories act as the commendation that reverberations through the lobbies of satire, denoting the persevering through soul of the individuals who devote their lives to making the world giggle.

8.1 Overcoming Writer's Block in Comedy

Beating a creative slump in parody is an impressive test that stands up to even the most prepared jokesters. The capacity to reliably produce new, entertaining, and unique material is integral to an entertainer's prosperity, and when the well of innovativeness dries up, it tends to be baffling and debilitating. This investigation digs into the idea of a creative slump in satire, the variables adding to its beginning, and methodologies for conquering this impressive snag to keep the comedic juices streaming.

Grasping the Idea of An inability to write:

A creative slump in satire, as in any imaginative pursuit, is a mind boggling peculiarity established in a combination of mental, profound, and outer elements. Jokesters might end up wrestling with an absence of motivation, self-question, apprehension about disappointment, or the strain to measure up to assumptions. It is fundamental to perceive that inability to write is a characteristic piece of the inventive flow and not a mark of inadequacy or an absence of ability.

Factors Adding to A creative slump in Satire:

A few variables add to the beginning of a creative slump in satire, each introducing its one of a kind arrangement of difficulties. One such variable is the assumption to continually convey new and interesting material. The strain to outperform past exhibitions or keep a specific degree of value can make a mind hindrance, frustrating the free progression of inventive thoughts. Outside stressors, private matters, or burnout can likewise obstruct the inventive flow, as the jokester's psychological energy becomes redirected.

Procedures for Conquering An inability to write:

1. **Embrace the Clear Page:**
   The scary clear page can be a wellspring of tension for some humorists confronting an inability to write. Rather than review it as an impediment, embrace the clear page as a material for possible jokes and thoughts. Allow yourself to compose openly without judgment, permitting the innovative strategy to normally unfurl.

2. **Change Your Current circumstance:**
   An adjustment of climate can frequently act as an impetus for getting through inability to write. Step beyond your standard composing space and track down motivation in another setting. Whether it's a recreation area, a café, or even an alternate room in

your home, an adjustment of landscape can animate imagination and deal a new point of view.

3. **Enjoy Reprieves and Rest:**
Comedic inventiveness is firmly connected to mental prosperity. While confronting an inability to write, it's vital to perceive the significance of enjoying reprieves and permitting your brain to rest. Participate in exercises that give you pleasure, whether it's perusing, watching parody specials, or basically going for a stroll. Resting the psyche frequently prompts recharged motivation.

4. **Freewriting and Conceptualizing:**
Participate in freewriting meetings where you permit your considerations to stream without agonizing over cognizance or construction. Put a clock and scribble down anything that rings a bell, regardless of whether it appears to be irrelevant or silly. Conceptualizing, either alone or with individual comics, can likewise start groundbreaking thoughts and viewpoints.

5. **Draw from Individual Encounters:**
The absolute best satire rises up out of private encounters and perceptions. On the off chance that creative slump endures, draw motivation from your own life, the eccentricities of your companions, or the quirks of regular circumstances. Legitimacy frequently reverberates with crowds, making individual material an important asset.

6. **Explore different avenues regarding Various Arrangements:**
Changing around the organization of your satire composing can break the repetitiveness and animate imagination. In the event that you commonly review stand schedules, take a stab at sketch composing or make a comedic character. Exploring different avenues regarding various configurations enhances your imaginative result as well as permits you to move toward humor from new points.

7. **Team up with Different Humorists:**
Joint effort can be a strong counteractant to an inability to write.

Draw in with individual humorists, run thoughts by one another, and share your battles. A new viewpoint from a colleague can give experiences, produce groundbreaking thoughts, and establish a strong climate where innovativeness can prosper.

8. **Put forth Reasonable Objectives:**
Separate your comedic composing objectives into more modest, more sensible errands. Putting forth practical objectives, for example, composing a specific number of jokes or premises every day, eases the mind-boggling pressure that adds to an inability to write. Celebrate little triumphs en route to keep up with inspiration.

9. **Examine and Gain from Past Exhibitions:**
Pondering past exhibitions can offer significant experiences into what worked and what didn't. Examine crowd responses, distinguish designs, and gain from the two triumphs and disappointments. This contemplative methodology can direct your future composition, assisting you with refining your comedic voice and style.

10. **Embrace Disappointment as a Learning An open door:**
Satire frequently includes experimentation. Embrace the chance of disappointment as a characteristic piece of the inventive flow. Only one out of every odd joke will land, and only one out of every odd thought will work out. Gaining from mishaps, changing your methodology, and keeping a versatile mentality are essential to conquering a creative slump.

11. **Look for Motivation Past Parody:**
Motivation can be tracked down in the most surprising spots. Investigate workmanship, writing, music, or some other type of inventiveness outside the domain of parody. Drawing motivation from assorted sources can implant your comedic composing with new points of view and one of a kind bits of knowledge.

12. **Practice Care and Unwinding Methods:**

Integrate care and unwinding methods into your daily practice to mitigate pressure and tension adding to an inability to write. Practices like contemplation, profound breathing, or yoga can make a psychological space helpful for inventiveness and assist with breaking the pattern of mental blockage.

1. Exercises to Spark Creativity

Flash inventiveness is a groundbreaking cycle that permits comics to get through mental hindrances, beat an inability to write, and create new, imaginative material. Similarly as actual activity is fundamental for keeping a sound body, innovative activities are essential for supporting a dynamic and creative psyche. This investigation digs into different activities intended to light imagination in jokesters, giving them a tool compartment to motivate groundbreaking thoughts, upgrade suddenness, and imbue their exhibitions with creativity.

1. **Word Affiliation Games:**
   Word affiliation games are a work of art and powerful method for invigorating innovative reasoning. Entertainers can begin with an irregular word and afterward unreservedly partner with different words that ring a bell. This exercise urges the cerebrum to make surprising associations and investigate new roads of thought. The subsequent word groups can act as prolific ground for creating jokes, premises, or even totally new comedic ideas.

2. **Ambiguity Activities:**
   Confusion, the component of shock or suddenness, is a foundation of humor. Jokesters can purposely compare irrelevant components, thoughts, or situations to make clever ambiguities. For instance, consolidating two apparently irrelevant ideas, for example, "talking creatures" and "new employee screenings," can prompt one of a kind and entertaining premises. This exercise empowers considering new ideas and embracing the ridiculous.

3. **Character Creation Studios:**
   Creating comedic characters is a superb activity to start innovativeness. Humorists can imagine fictitious people with particular qualities, characteristics, and points of view. These characters can then be set in different situations or given explicit difficulties. Investigating the world through the eyes of these characters frequently yields surprising and clever bits of knowledge, improving the comic's comedic tool kit.

4. **Continuous flow Composing:**
   Continuous flow composing includes writing down considerations and thoughts really mind without separating or altering. Jokesters can save devoted time for freestyle composing, permitting their considerations to stream without judgment. This exercise is especially successful for beating self-control and getting to crude, unfiltered inventiveness. The objective isn't cleaned material yet rather an unconstrained investigation of thoughts.

5. **Visual Improvements and Picture Affiliations:**
   Inventiveness can be started by visual upgrades. Entertainers can gather various pictures, whether photos, delineations, or irregular visuals, and use them as prompts for creating comedic thoughts. Partner humor with pictures can prompt unforeseen associations and trigger innovative storylines or zingers.

6. **Comedy Games and Activities:**
   Improvisational activities and games are basic apparatuses for starting imagination in comics. Whether taking part in bunch comedy meetings or rehearsing solo activities, spontaneous creation encourages suddenness and speedy reasoning. Games like "Indeed, And..." and "Single word Story" challenge entertainers to expand on one another's thoughts, cultivating a cooperative and imaginatively invigorating climate.

7. **Reevaluation of Regular Situations:**
   Taking ordinary, regular situations and reevaluating them through a comedic focal point is a fantastic activity for igniting

imagination. Joke artists can choose common circumstances, like sitting tight in line or looking for food, and infuse humor by overstating, mocking, or adding unforeseen components. This exercise empowers the investigation of humor in the standard.

8. **Figuring out Humor:**

Breaking down existing jokes or comedic situations and afterward figuring out them can be a strong activity. Comics can separate jokes into their parts, distinguish the arrangement, ambiguity, and zinger, and afterward reproduce them in exceptional ways. This picking apart interaction gives experiences into the mechanics of humor and moves the formation of unique comedic material.

9. **Ludicrous Associations:**

Making silly associations between inconsequential ideas or items is an activity that inspires bigger thoughts. Joke artists can move themselves to connect two apparently contradictory thoughts and track down humor in the silliness of their affiliation. This exercise empowers parallel reasoning and the revelation of sur-prising comedic points.

10. **Talk Mashup:**

Comics can take selections from popular talks, film exchanges, or verifiable discourses and remix them to make a comedic mashup. This exercise utilizes the imaginative muscles as well as includes recontextualizing recognizable substance into a silly story. The subsequent speech mashup can act as a wellspring of motivation for unique comedic composing.

11. **Turned off Inventiveness Meetings:**

Separating from computerized gadgets and embracing turned off imagination meetings can cultivate a more profound association with one's viewpoints. Jokesters can save devoted time away from screens, interruptions, and warnings to zero in on imaginative investigation.

This exercise considers a more careful and vivid commitment with thoughts, preparing for natural innovativeness to prosper.

12. Randomized Prompts and Limitations:

Randomized prompts and imperatives bring a component of unconventionality into the innovative approach. Jokesters can utilize devices like word generators, irregular sentence prompts, or requirements like restricting themselves to a specific word count or time span. These impediments force the psyche to think and react quickly and energize inventive arrangements.

b. Learning from Setbacks

Gaining from misfortunes is an innate and critical part of a comic's excursion, a cycle that shapes their art as well as characterizes their versatility and development inside the unusual universe of parody. Mishaps, whether as tepid crowd reactions, fizzled zingers, or a periodic besieging in front of an audience, are unavoidable in a field where achievement is in many cases estimated in giggling. This investigation digs into the significant meaning of difficulties in satire, the important illustrations they grant, and how comics can change difficulty into an impetus for development and achievement.

1. **Embracing Disappointment as an Ally to Progress:**
   Parody, similar to any work of art, is a territory where achievement and disappointment coincide. Comics who embrace disappointment as an inborn ally to progress take on an outlook that positions misfortunes as any open doors for advancing instead of marks of deficiency. In the steadily changing scene of humor, where crowd responses can be erratic, perceiving the cooperative connection among progress and disappointment is an essential move toward a comic's development.

2. **Investigating Crowd Elements:**
   Misfortunes in parody frequently brief jokesters to break down crowd elements with an insightful eye. A standard that crashes and burns may not really be a consequence of unfortunate material yet rather a bungle between the comic's style and the crowd's

inclinations. Jokesters who view mishaps as data of interest for understanding crowd subtleties can adjust their methodology, fitting their exhibitions to more readily reverberate with different groups.

3. **Refining Material Through Cycle:**

   Misfortunes as ineffective zingers or inadequately got jokes act as signs for material refinement. Comics can move toward difficulties as solicitations to repeat and develop their material. By calibrating jokes, changing timing, and exploring different avenues regarding conveyance, humorists change difficulties into a consistent course of sharpening their art. The iterative idea of satire takes into consideration consistent refinement and improvement.

4. **Exploring the Unconventionality of Humor:**

   Humor is innately emotional and eccentric, making mishaps a vital piece of an entertainer's excursion. Entertainers who gain from misfortunes perceive the ease of humor, understanding that what works in a single setting may not resound in another. By exploring the flighty idea of humor, comics foster a flexible range of abilities that empowers them to interface with assorted crowds and adjust to various comedic conditions.

5. **Creating Versatility and Steadiness:**

   Difficulties in satire act as pots for creating flexibility and determination. Entertainers who face the difficulties of quietness, aloofness, or even incidental irritating with effortlessness and constancy arise more grounded and stronger. The capacity to return from mishaps, as opposed to being deflected by them, is a sign of fruitful entertainers who explore the ups and downs of the satire scene.

6. **Building a Novel Comic Persona:**

   Misfortunes can push joke artists to reconsider their comedic persona and style. A joke that crashes and burns may be a chance to reevaluate whether it lines up with the entertainer's credible voice. By thinking about mishaps, entertainers can refine their comedic persona, guaranteeing it stays certifiable and particular. The method involved with building a novel comic persona is a continuous excursion molded by misfortunes and the resulting variations.

7. **Looking for Useful Input:**
Misfortunes make openings for humorists to look for productive criticism. Whether from friends, guides, or believed crowd individuals, productive criticism gives important bits of knowledge into what worked, what didn't, and regions for development. Comics who effectively look for criticism from different sources show a guarantee to ceaseless learning and development, transforming difficulties into venturing stones toward greatness.

8. **Developing Versatility:**
The capacity to adjust to various comedic settings and answer mishaps with adaptability is a sign of prepared comics. Misfortunes can emerge from factors unchangeable as far as a comic might be concerned, like startling disturbances or testing crowd socioeconomics. Joke artists who develop versatility view mishaps as any open doors to refine their flexibility abilities, guaranteeing they can explore different execution situations with beauty and readiness.

9. **Learning the Specialty of Timing:**
Misfortunes frequently highlight the meaning of timing in satire. A very much created joke conveyed with unfortunate timing can crash and burn, while an impeccably coordinated zinger can inspire boisterous giggling. Comics who gain from mishaps perceive the many-sided dance of timing in satire, refining their conveyance to expand comedic influence. The dominance of timing changes difficulties into illustrations that lift an entertainer's stage presence and comedic accuracy.

10. **Adjusting Dread and Fortitude:**
Mishaps can be scary, setting off a feeling of dread toward disappointment or self-question. Notwithstanding, jokesters who

face misfortunes with mental fortitude, recognizing the intrinsic dangers of their specialty, track down strength in weakness. Adjusting dread and boldness permits comics to explore difficulties with a versatile soul, changing mishaps into potential open doors for self-disclosure and self-awareness.

11. **Observing Little Triumphs:**

Despite difficulties, perceiving and celebrating little triumphs becomes fundamental for a humorist's spirit. A very much planned joke that evokes giggling, a shrewd spontaneous creation, or an effective transformation to a startling test — this large number of minutes, regardless of how little, add to a comic's excursion. Celebrating little triumphs fabricates certainty, cultivating a positive mentality that energizes flexibility despite difficulties.

12. **Encouraging a Development Mentality:**

Difficulties are basic parts of a development mentality. Humorists who embrace mishaps as pathways to development develop a mentality that values learning and improvement over fixed ideas of progress or disappointment. A development outlook empowers entertainers to see difficulties as transitory misfortunes instead of unrealistic obstructions, cultivating a persistent obligation to refining their specialty.

8.2 Celebrating Successes

Praising achievements in the realm of satire is an upbeat and critical piece of a jokester's excursion, denoting the achievements, wins, and snapshots of acknowledgment that intersperse the frequently difficult scene of humor. Triumphs, whether large or little, act as confirmations of a jokester's ability, flexibility, and association with crowds. This investigation dives into the significant meaning of praising triumphs in satire, the different structures these victories can take, and how they add to an entertainer's development, inspiration, and persevering through enthusiasm for the craft of making individuals chuckle.

1. **Recognizing Self-improvement:**
   Praising triumphs in satire frequently includes recognizing the self-awareness that goes with a humorist's excursion. Progressions in stage presence, conveyance, and the capacity to interface with different crowds are achievements that mirror an entertainer's developing range of abilities. Perceiving and praising these unpretentious yet significant changes add to a feeling of achievement and build up the obligation to nonstop improvement.

2. **Perceiving Imaginative Achievements:**
   Imaginative achievements, whether the improvement of another joke, the effective execution of a zinger, or the production of a vital person, address huge triumphs in a humorist's specialty.
   The method involved with perceiving and commending these innovative accomplishments cultivates a positive and spurred outlook. It urges comics to push their inventive limits, face challenges, and investigate creative ways to deal with humor.

3. **Embracing Positive Crowd Responses:**
   Positive crowd responses, like chuckling, acclaim, and certifiable commitment, are obvious markers of progress in satire. Praising these minutes includes delighting in the delight of interfacing with a group of people, evoking veritable giggling, and having an enduring impression. The energy traded among jokester and crowd turns into a strong wellspring of inspiration and powers the craving to keep making snapshots of shared chuckling.

4. **Remembering Fruitful Exhibitions:**
   Each fruitful presentation, whether on a little open mic stage or an excellent satire club, is a reason for festivity. Celebrating effective exhibitions includes savoring the experience, appreciating the positive input, and treasuring the recollections made in front of an audience. These festivals become standards of a jokester's excursion, helping them to remember the extraordinary force of giggling and the novel association fashioned with every crowd.

5. **Getting Acknowledgment and Grants:**

   Outside acknowledgment, like honors, awards, or solicitations to renowned parody celebrations, is an unmistakable type of progress that merits festivity. These affirmations approve a humorist's ability and commitments to the satire scene. Celebrating such accomplishments brings a feeling of achievement as well as fills in as a persuasive signal, moving humorists to arrive at new levels in their vocations.

6. **Exploring Misfortunes with Elegance:**

   Praising accomplishments in satire reaches out past unmistakable accomplishments to envelop the capacity to explore misfortunes with effortlessness and strength. Prevailing over difficulties, beating self-question, and persevering notwithstanding affliction are huge triumphs by their own doing. Jokesters who approach mishaps with a positive mentality and a pledge to development commend the actual excursion, perceiving that flexibility is an intrinsic type of progress.

7. **Building a Strong Parody People group:**

   The fellowship and backing inside the parody local area are in many cases ignored however vital parts of achievement. Commending triumphs includes recognizing the job of individual entertainers, coaches, and strong crowds in encouraging a feeling of local area. Whether through shared giggling, cooperative ventures, or the securities manufactured down and dirty of open mics, constructing and praising a strong satire local area upgrades the delight of progress.

8. **Cultivating a Positive Outlook:**

   Praising victories adds to the development of a positive outlook, a strong power that pushes humorists forward. Victories, regardless of how unobtrusive, act as confirmations of skill, powering fearlessness and a confidence in one's comedic capacities. A positive mentality turns into a main thrust that improves exhibitions as well as draws in additional victories through a hopeful and tough viewpoint.

9. **Moving Future Undertakings:**

Every festival of outcome in satire turns into a wellspring of motivation for future undertakings. Whether it's refining material, investigating new comedic styles, or chasing after bigger stages, recognizing past triumphs spurs joke artists to point higher and adventure into unfamiliar domains. Praising victories turns into a recurrent cycle, each win establishing the groundwork for the following inventive pursuit.

10. **Fortifying the Bond with Crowds:**

The common experience of chuckling makes an interesting connection among jokesters and their crowds. Commending victories includes perceiving the effect of this association, encouraging a feeling of shared delight, and reinforcing the bond with crowds. The festival turns into a corresponding trade, with crowds valuing the comics' gifts and humorists offering thanks for the chuckling and support.

11. **Adjusting Lowliness and Pride:**

Commending victories requires a fragile harmony among lowliness and pride. While recognizing accomplishments, entertainers who stay humble comprehend that progress in parody is a continuous excursion. Adjusting lowliness and pride includes valuing the awards without failing to focus on the persistent learning and development that describe the comedic make.

12. **Supporting Enthusiasm for Parody:**

Praising triumphs supports the enthusiasm for parody, mixing the fine art with euphoria, satisfaction, and a feeling of direction. The snapshots of festivity, whether private reflections or imparted merriments to individual jokesters, become standards that reignite the flash of enthusiasm. Supporting this energy guarantees that joke artists stay focused on the quest for giggling, even notwithstanding difficulties.

1. Recognizing Audience Reactions

Perceiving crowd responses is a work of art inside the fine art of satire, a complicated dance among entertainer and onlooker that significantly shapes the outcome of a comedic execution.

The giggling, acclaim, and, surprisingly, an intermittent quiet are nuanced reactions that act as quick input, directing joke artists through the steadily moving scene of humor. This investigation dives into the significant meaning of perceiving crowd responses, the different prompts comics explore, and how a sharp familiarity with these reactions lifts the specialty, changing a simple set into a dynamic and intuitive comedic experience.

1. **The Giggling Range:**
   Giggling, the heartbeat of parody, exists on a range that reaches from respectful laughs to loud roars. Perceiving the subtleties of chuckling includes knowing certified entertainment from well mannered kindness. Entertainers capable at perusing the chuckling range change their timing, conveyance, and material in view of the crowd's reaction, guaranteeing an agreeable trade of humor that reverberates with different preferences and sensibilities.

2. **The Force of Adulation:**
   Commendation is an instinctive articulation of endorsement and happiness, an aggregate affirmation from the crowd that rises above individual chuckling. Jokesters who perceive the force of commendation use it as an indicator of their association with the crowd. Convenient commendation fills in as a signal to expand on effective minutes, while the shortfall of praise prompts humorists to recalibrate and draw in the crowd in various ways.

3. **Exploring Quiet:**
   Quiet, however apparently perplexing, is an intense pointer that requires sharp translation. Jokesters who explore quiet with artfulness remember it as an open door instead of a misfortune.

Whether purposeful stops for comedic impact or minutes requiring crowd reflection, very much planned quietness turns into a device for pacing and accentuation, permitting comics to direct the crowd through the recurring pattern of chuckling.

4. **Recognizing Interesting Minutes:**
Crowd responses frequently uncover the appeal of comedic material. Recognizing minutes where the crowd resounds most firmly — maybe with shared encounters, social references, or widespread insights — empowers humorists to focus on the substance of association. Perceiving these interesting minutes cultivates a feeling of fellowship, changing the exhibition into a common encounter that rises above the stage.

5. **Changing Speed and Energy:**
Comics gifted at perceiving crowd responses grasp the significance of pacing and energy. The back and forth movement of giggling direct the beat of an exhibition. Whether speeding up the speed to exploit high-energy minutes or dialing back for unobtrusive subtleties, entertainers who adjust themselves to the crowd's reaction excel at conveying an exhibition that feels custom fitted to the extraordinary elements of each group.

6. **Measure of Commitment:**
Crowd responses act as a measure of commitment, giving important experiences into the mindfulness of the group. Comics who perceive indications of commitment — inclining forward, gesturing, or keeping in touch — jump all over the chance to fabricate a more cozy association. Changing conveyance in light of the degree of commitment guarantees that the comedic account stays enthralling and full.

7. **Perusing Looks:**
Past perceptible responses, looks offer a visual material that mirrors the crowd's personal process. Humorists skilled at perusing looks can measure a scope of feelings, from entertainment to shock or even consideration. This nuanced mindfulness permits

entertainers to tailor their presentation, utilizing facial prompts to upgrade comedic influence and close to home reverberation.

8. **Answering Irritating:**
Irritating, a flighty aspect of live exhibitions, requests quick and discerning reactions from humorists. Perceiving the subtleties of irritating — whether it comes from perky chat or authentic disturbance — enables humorists to explore these collaborations with mind and control. A deft reaction to harassing can change an expected disturbance into an extra layer of humor that resounds with the crowd.

9. **Moving Elements in Assorted Settings:**
Comics who perceive crowd responses ace the capacity to explore moving elements in different settings. Various scenes, societies, and socioeconomics add to one of a kind crowd reactions. Jokesters who remain sensitive to these varieties can adjust their material and conveyance, guaranteeing that humor rises above social hindrances and reverberates with crowds across a range of foundations.

10. **Building Association through Callbacks:**
Perceiving crowd responses permits comics to construct an association through callbacks — references to prior minutes in the exhibition that resound with the crowd. Callbacks make a feeling of congruity, compensating mindful audience members and building up the common experience. Jokesters who capably mesh callbacks into their schedules improve the generally comedic effect and cultivate a more profound association with the crowd.

11. **Using Non-Verbal Prompts:**
Non-verbal prompts, for example, non-verbal communication and motions, offer unobtrusive signs that entertainers can use to upgrade their exhibitions. Perceiving these signals empowers jokesters to use rawness for comedic impact, adding layers of humor that supplement verbal conveyance. Whether through

expressive looks or dynamic developments, talented jokesters utilize non-verbal signals to enhance the effect of their material.

12. **Encouraging a Cooperative Climate:**

At last, perceiving crowd responses changes the presentation into a cooperative trade. Comics who see the crowd as dynamic members instead of latent onlookers make a climate where chuckling turns into a common language. This cooperative methodology empowers crowd commitment, making every exhibition an extraordinary and intuitive comedic experience.

b. Refining and Improving Your Craft

Refining and working on one's specialty in the domain of parody is a ceaseless excursion, a unique cycle that requests devotion, mindfulness, and a resolute obligation to development. Whether a beginner jokester sharpening their most memorable set or a carefully prepared entertainer looking to raise their material, the quest for refinement is natural for the consistently developing scene of humor. This investigation dives into the significant meaning of refining and working on the comedic create, the complex roads through which jokesters can upgrade their abilities, and the getting through remunerations that originate from a persistent obligation to imaginative development.

1. **Craftsmanship of Jokes and Zingers:**
   At the center of comedic refinement lies the craftsmanship of jokes and zingers. Jokesters should carefully dissect the construction, timing, and conveyance of their material. Each word, interruption, and expression adds to the comedic design. By taking apart and recreating jokes, entertainers refine the accuracy of their zingers, guaranteeing greatest effect and reverberation with different crowds.

2. **The Craft of Timing:**
   Timing is the heartbeat of satire, a sensitive dance that isolates a very much coordinated zinger from a botched an open door.

Jokesters focused on refining their specialty perceive the craft of timing as a nuanced expertise that requires persistent adjustment. Dominating the nuances of pacing, stops, and cadence hoists exhibitions, changing them into orchestras of chuckling directed by the director's exact timing.

3. **Association with the Crowd:**

Refining the specialty includes developing a significant association with the crowd. Humorists who perceive the cooperative connection among entertainer and onlooker refine their capacity to check crowd responses. This elevated mindfulness takes into consideration ongoing changes, guaranteeing that material resounds truly and profoundly with the remarkable elements of each group.

4. **Versatility to Assorted Settings:**

The capacity to adjust to different settings is a sign of comedic refinement. Whether acting in close clubs, broad theaters, or whimsical scenes, entertainers should fit their material to suit the air. The expertise of adjusting to various settings requires a sharp comprehension of crowd elements, pacing, and the subtleties that make every exhibition unmistakable.

5. **Consolidating Self-awareness:**

Comedic refinement is indistinguishable from self-awareness. Entertainers who set out on an excursion of self-revelation mix their material with credible bits of knowledge and points of view. The developing idea of individual encounters turns into a wellspring of comedic motivation, considering material that reflects certifiable development and development after some time.

6. **Trial and error and Hazard Taking:**

Genuine refinement arises through trial and error and chance taking. Joke artists who try to push limits, investigate new comedic styles, and adventure into strange domains refine their specialty by embracing the unexplored world. The readiness to face challenges energizes imagination, encouraging a rich embroidery of material that rises above traditional limits.

7. **Input and Helpful Analysis:**
Looking for input and helpful analysis is an essential part of refinement. Jokesters who effectively request input from companions, tutors, and even crowd individuals gain significant experiences into what works and regions that request improvement. Helpful analysis fills in as a compass, directing entertainers toward a way of nonstop development and refinement.

8. **Composing and Revamping:**
The specialty of parody is indistinguishable from the art of composing and reworking. Comics focused on refinement comprehend that the main draft is just a beginning stage. The method involved with returning to, reexamining, and sharpening material is a tenacious quest for flawlessness. Every emphasis refines the comedic account, refining it to its substance and expanding its effect.

9. **Rawness and Stage Presence:**
Refinement stretches out past verbal conveyance to include rawness and stage presence. Jokesters perceive the force of non-verbal communication, looks, and development as necessary parts of comedic articulation. By refining these parts of execution, jokesters lift their capacity to enamor crowds outwardly, adding layers of humor to supplement their verbal mind.

10. **Embracing Disappointment as an Educator:**
Disappointment, as opposed to a misfortune, turns into a strong educator in the excursion of refinement. Entertainers who embrace disappointment as a characteristic piece of the inventive strategy learn priceless examples.
Every slip up turns into a chance to investigate, change, and arise more grounded. The versatility fashioned through embracing disappointment adds to an entertainer's continuous development and refinement.

11. **Cooperative Learning and Systems administration:**
    The quest for refinement is certainly not a singular undertaking yet a cooperative educational experience. Comics who effectively participate in systems administration, team up with peers, and take part in parody networks establish a climate helpful for shared development. Gaining according to different points of view and encounters refines a's comprehension comic might interpret humor and widens their comedic collection.

12. **Authority of the Erratic:**

Comedic refinement is inadequate without the authority of the unusual. The live idea of satire requests a capacity to explore startling disturbances, bothering, or abrupt changes in crowd elements. Jokesters who refine their specialty to incorporate improvisational abilities and a quiet, made disposition notwithstanding capriciousness arise as bosses of their art.

Chapter 9

Conclusion

In the many-sided embroidered artwork of comedic articulation, the investigation of Comedic Material Canvas has disclosed the significant transaction among chuckling and narrating, winding around together the strings of humor to make dynamic, reminiscent accounts that resound across societies and time. From the rich legacy of comedic customs to the contemporary subtleties of stand-up, parody, and droll, the brushstrokes on this comedic material have enlightened the assorted structures and styles that inspire giggling and enlighten the human experience.

The excursion through the comedic scene has crossed the mental domains of humor, revealing the complexities of giggling, the advantages it gives to people and society, and the hidden systems that make us chuckle. Digging into the domains of setting the stage, making critical characters, and plotting for chuckles, we've investigated the careful imaginativeness associated with making comedic stories that enthrall and engage. From offbeat characters to immortal comedic prime examples, the characters painted on this material are a demonstration of the inventiveness and innovativeness that inject humor with profundity and appeal.

Inspecting the semantic components of making comical exchange, utilizing wit and plays on words, and dominating timing and conveyance, we've taken apart the phonetic range that joke artists ably use to bring out chuckling. The specialty of humor, complicatedly woven with social subtleties and cultural reflections, reverberates through parody, observational satire, and the investigation of restrictions, introducing an intricate, powerful scene that mirrors the steadily moving shapes of cultural standards.

The excursion has been an ensemble of giggling, from the arrangement and bend to the zinger, each note painstakingly organized to evoke happiness and shock. Investigating the profundities of motivation drawn from individual encounters, disasters transformed into humor, and observational satire established in sharp bits of knowledge, we've stripped back the layers of the human experience to uncover the comedic gold secret inside our day to day existences.

The language of chuckling, communicated through playing with words, risqué remark, allusion, and embracing ludicrousness, mirrors the flexibility and versatility of humor across social scenes. Dreamlike and strange humor, offset with an investigation of dull parody and the almost negligible difference among humor and offense, exhibit the broadness and profundity of the comedic material. Creating a comedic voice, fostering an extraordinary style, and exploring social responsive qualities enlighten the imaginativeness engaged with guaranteeing that humor rises above limits while regarding different points of view.

Chasing comedic greatness, we've explored the difficulties and wins that accentuate a comic's excursion, investigated techniques to conquer an inability to write, participated in activities to ignite imagination, and gained from mishaps. Praising triumphs, perceiving crowd responses, and refining the specialty have arisen as the cornerstones of an entertainer's continuous odyssey, an excursion that interlaces strength, versatility, and an immovable obligation to making individuals giggle.

All in all, the comedic material is a no nonsense demonstration of the widespread force of giggling — a power that rises above language, culture, and time. As we consider the complexities of humor, the different structures it takes, and the significant effect it has on people and society, we end up remaining at the intersection of creative articulation and shared euphoria. The brushstrokes on this comedic material recount stories, incite thought, and help us to remember the magnificence intrinsic in tracking down humor in the woven artwork of our lives. With each stroke, humorists make giggling as well as associations, cultivating a common human encounter that reverberates a long ways past the stage, screen, or composed word. The comedic material, always advancing and growing, welcomes us to keep investigating, giggling, and finding the boundless conceivable outcomes inside the domain of humor.

9.1 The Ever-Evolving Landscape of Comedy

The consistently developing scene of parody is a unique material, continually molded and reshaped by the flows of social movements, cultural changes, and the endless walk of time. Parody, as a work of art, has a surprising skill to adjust, reflect, and challenge the overall standards of its period. This investigation digs into the complex elements of satire's development, following its excursion from old roots to current appearances, and featuring the manners by which humor has turned into a permanent reflection of the human experience.

Parody's foundations stretch profound into artifact, stringing through the old civilizations of Greece and Rome. The dramatic virtuoso of Aristophanes in antiquated Athens laid the basis for comedic customs that would reverberate through the passageways of time. The comedic material of bygone eras frequently portrayed the weaknesses of people, ridiculing cultural designs, and offering a soothing delivery for crowds wrestling with the intricacies of presence.

As time spread out its story, the Renaissance time frame introduced a recovery of comedic expressions. Crafted by William Shakespeare, with plays like "Twelfth Evening" and "A Midsummer Night's Fantasy," exhibited the immortal idea of humor, fit for rising above worldly limits and resounding across hundreds of years. Satire, during this age, turned into a vehicle for investigating human indiscretion, love, and the idiocies of the human condition.

The approach of film in the twentieth century slung parody onto another stage, both in a real sense and metaphorically. The quiet film time, set apart by the droll jokes of Charlie Chaplin and Buster Keaton, presented a visual language of humor that rose above phonetic boundaries. Droll satire, with its overstated genuineness and visual gags, turned into a general language, joining crowds in giggling regardless of their local tongues.

The mid-twentieth century saw the ascent of stand-up parody, a class that brought the closeness of humor straightforwardly to the crowd. Jokesters like Lenny Bruce, George Carlin, and Richard Pryor upset satire by digging into social and political discourse, testing cultural standards, and pushing the limits of what was viewed as satisfactory in front of an audience. This time denoted a shift from the simply dreamer nature of satire to a device for cultural contemplation and study.

The late twentieth and mid 21st hundreds of years saw the multiplication of elective satire structures. Comedy parody, spearheaded by bunches like The Subsequent City and improvisational shows like "Whose Line Is It In any case?," added a layer of immediacy and crowd cooperation to the comedic scene. In the interim, the computerized age birthed another boondocks for satire with the appearance of online stages. Jokesters tracked down a worldwide crowd through YouTube, webcasts, and online entertainment, testing the conventional watchmen of media outlets.

The variety of comedic articulation extended further with the rise of elective voices, frequently testing winning standards and supporting for civil rights. Entertainers like Margaret Cho, Wanda Sykes, and Hannah Gadsby utilized their foundation to defy issues of race, orientation, and sexuality, reshaping the comedic scene into a more comprehensive and intelligent space.

The direction of satire isn't just set apart by the advancement of its structures yet in addition by the moving elements of cultural sensibilities. As social perspectives change, satire turns into a mirror that reflects, questions, and develops with the times. The humor that was satisfactory in one period may be thought of as obsolete or hostile in another. The steadily developing scene requests a consistent reassessment of comedic standards, pushing entertainers to explore the barely recognizable difference between pushing limits and regarding responsive qualities.

Also, the globalized idea of amusement has prompted multifaceted preparation of comedic styles. Entertainers from different social foundations carry their one of a kind points of view to the very front, enhancing the worldwide comedic embroidery with a rich mosaic of voices. The once-prevailing Western-driven perspective on parody has given way to a more pluralistic, interconnected comedic world.

In this steadily moving scene, the job of parody as a social editorial device has become progressively articulated. Entertainers, furnished with mind and knowledge, draw in with squeezing cultural issues, testing standards, and offering a focal point through which crowds can see and consider the world. Parody, a type of satire established in study, has turned into a strong vehicle for considering power structures responsible, addressing authority, and igniting exchange.

As we explore the mind boggling territory of the 21st hundred years, satire keeps on developing because of the difficulties and wins of our times. The worldwide network worked with by the web, the democratization of content creation, and the ascent of different voices have pushed parody into a period of exceptional dynamism. The comedic material, once restricted to stages and screens, presently spreads across virtual scenes, making a computerized public square where comics and crowds take part in a continuous discourse that rises above geological lines.

9.2 Encouragement for Aspiring Comedic Writers

For trying comedic essayists, the excursion into the universe of humor is both an elating experience and a significant investigation of the human experience. As you set out on this way, it's fundamental to perceive that the domain of parody is all around as different as the bunch ways individuals see and express chuckling. Whether you are attracted to stand-up, sketch composing, sitcoms, or some other comedic structure, here is a guide of consolation to direct you through the exhilarating, at times testing, yet continuously remunerating landscape of comedic composing.

1. **Embrace Your Novel Voice:**
   In the tremendous embroidery of comedic articulation, your voice is the brushstroke that adds a particular shade. Embrace your uniqueness and let your voice radiate through your composition. Whether your humor is clever, disrespectful, or crazy, genuineness resounds with crowds. Your point of view is exceptional, and the world requirements to hear it.

2. **Gain from the Bosses:**
   Comedic composing has a rich genealogy of bosses who have made a permanent imprint on the specialty. Concentrate on crafted by comedic legends, from Imprint Twain and P.G. Wodehouse to current symbols like Tina Fey and Dave Chappelle. Dissect their composing strategies, timing, and the inconspicuous craft of catching the human experience through humor. Gain from the best, however make sure to imbue your special flavor in with the general mish-mash.

3. **Peruse Generally and Diversely:**
   Comedic motivation can be tracked down in the most startling spots. Peruse generally and diversely to open yourself to various composing styles, classes, and points of view. Whether it's exemplary writing, contemporary books, or even funny cartoons, different perusing expands your comedic range and permits you to draw motivation from different sources.

4. **Compose Routinely and Boldly:**
   Composing is a muscle that fortifies with standard activity. Put away devoted time for composing, regardless of whether it's only

a couple of moments daily. Go ahead and try different things with various comedic styles and topics. Valor in your composing is the impetus for finding your comedic reach and refining your voice.

5. **Notice the World with a Comedic Focal point:**
Comedic motivation frequently prowls in the regular snapshots of life. Notice your general surroundings with a comedic focal point. Track down humor in the ordinary, the crazy, and the inconsistencies of human way of behaving. Change perceptions into comedic gold by infusing your extraordinary viewpoint and discourse.

6. **Embrace Disappointment as a Venturing Stone:**
Few out of every odd joke will land, and few out of every odd comedic piece will be a show-stopper. Embrace disappointment as a fundamental piece of the inventive approach. Every stumble is an illustration, a refining instrument that levels up your abilities. Be encouraged by difficulties; all things being equal, view them as venturing stones on the way to comedic dominance.

7. **Look for Useful Criticism:**
Composing is a lone undertaking, however the excursion to comedic greatness benefits according to outside points of view. Look for useful criticism from companions, guides, or composing gatherings. Helpful analysis is an important compass that guides you toward areas of progress while reinforcing your assets. Embrace criticism as a cooperative device for development.

8. **Foster Your Feeling of Timing:**
Timing is the heartbeat of satire. Whether it's the cadence of a zinger or the pacing of a comedic story, sharpening your feeling of timing is significant. Focus on what your words land and the mean for they have on the peruser's or alternately crowd's insight. Authority of timing changes great satire into something genuinely extraordinary.

9. **Be Available to Joint effort:**
Satire frequently flourishes in cooperative conditions. Be available

to working with different scholars, entertainers, or entertainers. Cooperative endeavors offer different viewpoints that would be useful, cultivating a rich innovative collaboration. The aggregate giggling created through coordinated effort can be more noteworthy than the amount of its parts.

10. **Remain Tough and Continue on:**
The way to comedic achievement is seldom direct. Dismissals, analysis, and snapshots of self-question are important for the excursion. Remain strong and persist through difficulties. The most celebrated comedic scholars confronted misfortunes however arose more grounded, outfitted with a flexibility that powered their prosperity.

11. **Continue Developing and Testing:**
Comedic composing is a unique work of art that develops with social movements and cultural changes. Remain receptive to the overall outlook, and go ahead and explore different avenues regarding new comedic styles. The readiness to advance guarantees that your parody stays new, pertinent, and full with crowds.

12. **Observe Your Successes, Of all shapes and sizes:**

Chasing comedic dominance, praise each success, whether it's a generally welcomed joke, a completed content, or a fruitful live presentation. Perceive and savor the delight in your achievements, of all shapes and sizes. Commending your successes powers your energy and supports your obligation to the comedic create.

9.3 Final Thoughts on the Laughter-Filled Journey

As we consider the giggling filled venture through the huge spread of comedic investigation, it becomes obvious that humor isn't simply a work of art however a general language that rises above limits and unites individuals.

This excursion has been an energetic embroidery woven with strings of mind, parody, and silliness, displaying the wealth and variety inborn in the realm of satire. As we track the comedic scene from its old roots to the contemporary phases of stand-up, online stages, and then some, the reverberating reverberations of giggling act as a demonstration of the getting through force of humor to interface, incite thought, and evoke delight.

In this giggling filled odyssey, we've investigated the bunch features of comedic articulation, seeing the development of comedic structures, the mental subtleties of chuckling, and the complicated imaginativeness engaged with creating humor. The material of parody, painted with strokes going from the inconspicuous to the strong, mirrors the intricacies of the human experience. From the immortal mind of exemplary writing to the unique suddenness of comedy parody, each structure adds to the multicolored scene of giggling.

The giggling filled venture has additionally dove into the profundities of humor's effect on people and society. Giggling, with its helpful characteristics, fills in as a medicine for the spirit, easing pressure, cultivating association, and giving a focal point through which we can explore life's difficulties with strength and effortlessness. Past the individual, parody arises as a social discourse instrument, a mirror that reflects cultural standards, challenges authority, and prompts thoughtfulness. Parody, observational satire, and the investigation of social subtleties add to a comedic discourse that rises above diversion to turn into a power for reflection and change.

In navigating the giggling filled scene, we've experienced a bunch of comedic structures, each with its unmistakable appeal and allure. Stand-up parody, with its crude credibility and the cozy association among entertainer and crowd, uncovers the weaknesses and idiocies of human life. Parody, a sharp-edged device, involves humor as a vehicle for scrutinize, rocking the boat and scrutinizing the overarching standards of the day. From the immortal allure of droll to the provocative stories of sitcoms, the variety inside parody guarantees that there is a flavor to suit each sense of taste.

The chuckling filled venture has likewise been a festival of the specialists who rejuvenate humor, the comics who, with their one of a kind voices, spellbinding exhibitions, and resolute obligation to making individuals snicker, become modelers of happiness. Their capacity to explore the consistently moving elements of crowd responses, to track down motivation in the unremarkable, and to implant their comedic stories with genuineness is a demonstration of the masterfulness inborn in the realm of parody.

As we bid goodbye to this giggling filled venture, it isn't just a decision yet a take-off point for the continuous investigation of humor's unlimited domains. The chuckling, accounts, and snapshots of funniness experienced en route act as enduring friends, tokens of the significant effect that satire has on the human soul. The comedic material, painted with grins and stories, welcomes us to keep unwinding its secrets, finding new types of jollity, and savoring the chuckling filled minutes that join us in shared bliss.

In these last contemplations on the chuckling filled venture, let us convey with us the grasping that, in the realm of satire, each zinger, each comedic contort, and each eruption of giggling is a festival of our common humankind. As we explore the eccentric scene of life, may we track down comfort and motivation in the persevering through force of humor — a power that rises above time, culture, and situation. The chuckling filled venture is an update that, in the excellent auditorium of presence, satire becomes the overwhelming focus, welcoming us to delight in the brilliant idiocies that make us human.